Lancashire

40 favourite Walks

The author and publisher have made every effort to ensure that the information in this publication is accurate, and accept no responsibility whatsoever for any loss, injury or inconvenience experienced by any person or persons whilst using this book.

published by
pocket mountains ltd
The Old Church, Annanside,
Moffat DG10 9HB

ISBN: 978-1-907025-761

Text and photography copyright © Alastair Ross 2021

The right of Alastair Ross to be identified as the Author of this work has been asserted by him in accordance with the Copyright, Designs and Patents Act 1988

A catalogue record for this book is available from the British Library

Contains Ordnance Survey data © Crown copyright and database 2021 supported by out of copyright mapping 1945-1961

Printed by J Thomson Colour Printers, Glasgow

Introduction

Don't underestimate Lancashire! Although it is one of the UK's most populous counties, it is also largely a rural one, including no less than three Areas of Outstanding Natural Beauty (AONB) and abutting the Pennines, Dales and Lake District. There is a huge variety of inspiring walking country, from the coast to hills and from forests to moors.

Walking country

Modern Lancashire lies at the heart of North West England, stretching from the edge of the Lake District to the borders of the great conurbations of Liverpool and Manchester. The county straddles the coastal plain and climbs to the high watershed of the Pennines. This range of hills, dividing Northern England, lies far nearer the Irish Sea than the North Sea, sometimes just a few miles from the west coast. Key transport corridors such as the West Coast Main Line and the M6 exploit the narrow coastal strip as successors to the packhorse and Roman routes that predate them.

The chapters in this book reflect the main regions of magnificent walking country in Lancashire. To the north the Arnside and Silverdale peninsula crosses the border with Cumbria. This AONB contains a range of low limestone hills, decked by native woodland and bordered by the saltmarsh fringe of Morecambe Bay. Nearby the picturesque Lune Valley weaves through pastoral countryside backed by the hills of Bowland and the Dales.

Inland, the countryside rises to the high Pennines and their foothills. The Forest of Bowland is not an area of woodland but an ancient royal hunting ground. Now an AONB it is one of the most remote areas in Northern England, containing only a few small villages and hamlets. Its large wedge of high moorland and fells, riven with deep valleys and clear flowing streams, offers an excellent habitat for birdlife, especially raptors.

The West Pennine Moors make up the third of Lancashire's AONBs. This swathe of wild moorland serves both as a retreat and an outdoor adventure hub for the mill towns and industrial centres such as Blackburn, Bolton, Bury and Accrington that surround it. Here, struggles for access rights long predate the famous Kinder Scout Trespass, with freedom to roam on Darwen Moor being gained as early as 1896. The wet climate has been exploited not only for cotton, but also for water supply, and the shores of its many reservoirs make for good walking loops.

The Ribble Valley divides Bowland from Pendle and East Lancashire. It's an area of lush farmland extending from the fringes of the Yorkshire Dales towards the salty estuary at Preston. Centred around the historic town of Clitheroe, there are also many pretty villages and riverside walks. Pendle Hill dominates the scene between Clitheroe and Burnley, an isolated whaleback ridge visible for many miles and once believed to be the highest hill in England. At less than 600m, it does not even make mountain 'status', but its brooding presence and dark historic associations far outweigh its vital statistics. Fine walks cross the top and explore the wooded fringes of the hill which is part of the Bowland AONB.

To the west stretches lower-lying land from the M6 to the coast. Between the Wyre and Ribble Estuaries the Fylde is largely flat farmland with a number of attractive market towns. The Fylde coastline is peppered with traditional seaside resorts, headed by legendary Blackpool, but it also has a history of fishing, notably at Fleetwood. The area south of the Ribble is the 'market garden of the North West', with production of all kinds of vegetables such as potatoes and leeks. There are many surprising charming nooks and crannies to be found, bound by the spectacular seascape at the county's western edge. Morecambe Bay and the estuaries of the Lune, Wyre, Ribble and Mersey provide fertile ground for migrating and native birds, geese and waders. The tidal range here is among the highest in the world, creating a vast world of intertidal sands, saltmarsh and sand dunes.

The southeastern corner of Lancashire, around Burnley and Rossendale, is part of the South Pennines which has no formal designation but is largely defined as the area between the Peak District and the Yorkshire Dales (much of it falling within West Yorkshire and Greater Manchester).

This is a remarkable walking area in itself and as such has its own separate volume, South Pennines: 40 Favourite Walks.

History

Lancashire's most famous symbol, the red rose, reflects the protracted medieval conflict known as the Wars of the Roses, but the county's history long predates these battles. The Romans established key towns such as Lancaster and Manchester in the area controlled by the British Brigantes tribe. After the Romans, the region eventually became part of the Anglo-Saxon kingdom of Northumbria. But it was not until 1182 that Lancashire was formally established with boundaries that stretched from the Mersey to the Duddon Estuary in the west of the Lake District.

During the Industrial Revolution the cities of Liverpool and Manchester mushroomed in size and importance, the former as a major Atlantic port with the ignominious title of being Britain's third slave-trading port, and the latter as a major manufacturing centre. Cotton and coal were two of the most significant economic drivers and the county processed over four-fifths of the world's cotton. Major towns grew in size and by the middle of the 20th century Lancashire was the most populous English county with more than five million Lancastrians living within its borders.

Lancaster's own river port was England's fourth colonial port during the 18th century, and many Lancastrian families made their fortunes as plantation owners, with the triangular trade based around transatlantic slavery bringing huge prosperity to the region. The legacy of this dark era is still visible in the Georgian civic architecture, some port street names and a few surviving country mansions.

Historically, North West England has been relatively remote from southern political dominance, lying across the Pennines, away from the main north-south route through Yorkshire. The region has looked west to Ireland and beyond and its political tradition has been tinged with radicalism. Chartists were strong in the mill towns and cities, demanding equal suffrage and participation for all men. The Peterloo Massacre in 1819 was a dramatic and shameful moment in a continuous struggle for recognition and equality.

Lancashire's more remote rural areas with the potential to harbour recusants and unorthodox practices were a continued source of unease for religious and political authority. It was from isolated rural farms around the base of Pendle Hill that a dozen women were seized and charged with witchcraft in the early 17th century in the Lancashire witch trials, spawned in a climate of fear and suspicion and culminating in the execution of the 'Pendle Witches' at Lancaster Castle in 1612.

Today's Lancashire is a very different shape from the original county that came about in the Middle Ages. Local government reorganisation in 1974 created the new metropolitan counties of Greater Manchester and Merseyside. The areas north of Morecambe Bay ('over the sands') augmented newly formed Cumbria, while a swathe of the West Riding of Yorkshire around the Forest of Bowland and West Craven was ceded to Lancashire to give it its current population of about 1.5 million.

Getting around

There is a comprehensive network of roads and motorways that connect the county north, south and east. But it is also possible to access most of the walks in this volume by public transport.

The West Coast Main Line runs the length of Lancashire with stations at Preston and Lancaster. Branches run across the Fylde to Blackpool, through East Lancashire to Burnley and Colne, and to Silverdale and Arnside. A further line connects Clitheroe with Blackburn, Bolton and Manchester, passing through the heart of the West Pennine Moors. Electric Merseyrail trains link Liverpool with Southport and Ormskirk (for Preston).

Regular buses serve most parts of the county. The exception is the Forest of Bowland, which has very few bus routes, reflecting and reinforcing its remoteness and isolation. Search online for Lancashire buses to find the council's index of timetables. Blackburn-with-Darwen and Blackpool are unitary authorities and have separate arrangements.

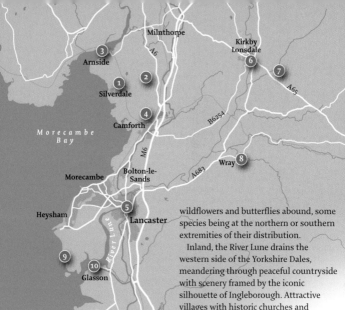

Milnthorpe

Kirkby
Lonsdale
⑥

⑦
A65

③
Arnside

②

A6

Silverdale
①

④
Camforth

B6254

*Morecambe
Bay*

M6

Bolton-le-
Sands
Morecambe

A683

Wray
⑧

Heysham

⑤
Lancaster

River Lune

⑨

⑩
Glasson

Northern Lancashire is flanked by the majestic peaks of the Lake District and bordered by the vast silvery sands of Morecambe Bay. Here the coastal plain contracts to become a strip of land between the hills and the sea, carrying ancient and modern routes between the north and south.

At the very northern edge of the county lies the remarkable limestone peninsula around Silverdale. Clad with ancient woodland and home to an extraordinary range of wildlife, the area is stewarded as the Arnside and Silverdale Area of Outstanding Natural Beauty and extends into neighbouring Cumbria. Birds,

wildflowers and butterflies abound, some species being at the northern or southern extremities of their distribution.

Inland, the River Lune drains the western side of the Yorkshire Dales, meandering through peaceful countryside with scenery framed by the iconic silhouette of Ingleborough. Attractive villages with historic churches and welcoming hostelries have been hewn out of the very landscape they have colonised. South of the Lune, the flat coastal mosslands are fringed by saltmarsh and are protected from inundation by the Irish Sea with embankments and drains. This is a very different kind of walking area, offering wide skies and distant views.

At the heart of it all lies the ancient city of Lancaster, guarding the lowest crossing of the Lune since Roman times. A maritime museum commemorates its seagoing past, including its darker history as a nerve centre for the slave trade. On the opposite side of the city, the elegant Ashton Memorial is a reminder of its Victorian commercial energy. There is plenty to explore.

Northern Lancashire

The woods and wells of Silverdale

Distance 11km **Time** 4 hours
Terrain field and woodland paths with
short stretches of stony foreshore and
one flight of rock steps at Wood Well
Map OS Explorer OL7 **Access** trains to
Silverdale Station

Silverdale is a captivating area of low
limestone hills, cloaked in oak woodland
and bordered by the vast tidal sands of
Morecambe Bay. This circuit offers
almost everything from coastal
landscape to limestone crags and
woodland. It also visits no less than
three of Silverdale's historic wells.

Go through the kissing gate at the back
of the Eaves Wood National Trust car park
and follow the path into the woods. At a
T-junction, go left towards Pepperpot and
The Cove. After about 500m, bear right at
a junction, following a white waymark,
and continuing uphill through oak, silver
birch and beech trees. At another
junction, turn right, signed for Pepperpot,

and meander gently uphill until a white
waymark indicates the route left. At the
far end of a clearing, the path makes a left
turn to gain the summit of King William's
Hill. The Pepperpot, crowning the top, is a
stone edifice built to commemorate the
diamond jubilee of Queen Victoria in 1887.

From the summit, descend by the same
route and then turn right (SP car park).
Almost immediately leave the outward
route and turn right again to follow a
woodland path weaving downhill to a
junction and a fingerpost just below it.
Turn right, heading for The Cove. The
path follows the wall and after 50m
reaches a lane. Keep almost straight ahead
and follow the right of way along a
sequence of tracks, driveways and
footpaths until you come to a road. Sidle
onto this, keeping straight ahead until the
road bends sharply to the right.

Turn left, taking Cove Lane to the shore
at the Cove, a small stony bay surrounded
by low-lying cliffs. Take the path up the

◄ Jenny Brown's Point

cliff to the left and continue across fields to Silverdale village, enjoying a wide panorama of Morecambe Bay. At the road, dogleg right and then left into Lindeth Road. In 700m the road turns left at Gibraltar Farm. Keep straight ahead on the no-through lane towards Jenny Brown's Point, passing Lindeth Tower. You can deviate off this road to the left, using a gate, to explore Jack Scout, an enticing area of gorse-clad cliff overlooking the bay.

At Brown's Houses, the path continues to the right of the building and along the rocky foreshore and later saltmarsh. A solitary chimney is all that remains of a copper-smelting enterprise. At a fingerpost, turn left for Heald Brow and Hollins Lane. A steep path winds uphill through bramble bushes and across the heath and fields at Heald Brow. Close to a wooden barn reach a walled lane, following this to the right to reach a road.

Almost opposite, take the left of the two footpaths to descend Wood Well Cliff. Walk along the base of the cliffs to Wood Well, a secluded dell, once a watering hole for drovers' cattle. A path ascends the cliff beyond, signed for The Green via cliff path. There is a short but steep section of rock steps, requiring some use of hands, and it may be slippery in wet weather. An interesting path traverses woodland to a

junction. Bear left for The Green, contouring the top of the cliff to come to a road. Turn right and walk along the road for 200m. At the junction by Rock Cottage, turn left for another 200m. Then turn right along a track (SP The Row), gradually descending to Burton Well. Continue across the water meadow beyond, soon turning right across a wooden footbridge. A gate leads into woodland and the path ascends to reach a lane. Turn left for 30m, then right for Dog Slack Well and The Row. A small limestone valley passes Dog Slack Well and an adjacent iron pump. Keep ahead through a gate, then amble through the trees until you meet a narrow lane at the Row. Turn right and follow the lane back to the car park.

Gait Barrows and Leighton Moss

Distance 10km **Time** 3 hours
Terrain mostly woodland tracks and
paths, may be muddy after rain
Map OS Explorer OL7 **Access** join the walk
at Silverdale Station, close to Leighton
Moss RSPB Reserve, 300m from the walk;
buses from Carnforth and Silverdale also
serve this point

**Explore two nature reserves and swathes
of ancient woodland. Leighton Moss is an
internationally important wetland
habitat managed by the RSPB, while the
National Nature Reserve at Gait Barrows
is a warren of woodland, limestone
pavement and marsh.**

There are a few roadside parking places
at the north end of Yealand Redmayne,
known as Yealand Storrs, near to the
junction of the roads to Arnside and
Silverdale. Take the footpath through a
gate between these two roads, signed for
Moss Lane and Haweswater. A track
traverses Yealand Hall Allotment, an area

of heathland with stunted trees and
brambles colonising the weathered
limestone pavement.

After 1km, go through a gate and turn
left along a walled lane to the entrance to
Gait Barrows. This National Nature
Reserve is home to a variety of flowers
and rare butterflies such as the High
Brown and Pearl-bordered fritillaries.
Cross over a couple of fields and then
trace the route curving around the right-
hand side of a marsh before bending back
to the right through a gateway. Meander
around the perimeter of another small
bog, before turning right through a gate.
A firm track now leads through coppiced
woodland to reach a road in about 700m.

Turn left and walk along the road for
about 300m before turning left onto a
footpath back into the reserve. A slight
descent along a small gully leads to a
T-junction in front of a wall. Turn left and
soon, by a small footbridge, turn right
through a gate marked 'Nature Trail'. The

permissive path leads along duckboards at the reedy edge of Hawes Water. At the far end of the reserve, keep ahead onto the road, Moss Lane, passing several cottages. Just before the lane rises to cross the railway, turn left through a gateway along a permissive track through the old limeworks area, curving to the left. Soon, at the top of a small rise, watch out for a footpath intersecting the route. Take this to the right, then cross the wall by a fingerpost to Storrs Lane. Cross Silverdale Golf Course, keeping a straight line marshalled by waymarks.

At the road, turn right for 200m, then turn left onto a bridleway to cross Leighton Moss RSPB Reserve on a public causeway. The visitor centre lies a further 300m along the road. The reserve includes the largest reedbed in North West Europe, home to otters, woodland birds and many waders. The public causeway crosses the reedbed and offers many glimpses over open water; there is an observation hide part of the way along it.

As the reedbed ends, the track rises to the farmyard at Grisedale, becoming a tarmac lane. Soon the buildings of Leighton Hall appear ahead, stately home of the Gillow family, the Lancaster-based furniture manufacturers. Before reaching the Hall, opposite Home Farm Cottage, turn left onto a footpath for Yealand Redmayne. Cross two fields to Deepdale Wood, then immediately take the right-hand fork (waymarked) to ascend the woods. When the path descends to a dip, look out for Deepdale Pond set in a hollow 200m to the right. Keep straight ahead, now rising again until the path passes through a wall gap and comes to a T-junction. Turn left for Round Top and Yealand Storrs, through Cringlebarrow Wood, for about 300m. As the path levels out, watch for an unmarked right-hand turning heading steeply downhill. Weave through the trees to return to Yealand Redmayne. At the road, turn left to return to the start.

Arnside Knott and the Kent Estuary

Distance 7km **Time** 2 hours 30
Terrain coastal footpaths or shoreline, followed by limestone paths with a steep and stony ascent and descent
Map OS Explorer OL7 **Access** trains to Arnside Station on the Lancaster-Barrow Line

Arnside Knott must be one of the most exciting small hills in Britain. Although only just over 500m high, it commands views over the vast sands of Morecambe Bay and the serrated heights of the Lake District. The Knott and its environs are a haven for all kinds of wildlife, flowers, birds and butterflies. Strictly speaking it is cheating to feature the Knott here as the entire walk is in Cumbria. However, Cumbria's Arnside and Lancashire's Silverdale are umbilically connected in a magical limestone peninsula and it would be a shame not to celebrate this whole Area of Outstanding Natural Beauty for the sake of observing county lines.

The high tidal range of Morecambe Bay generates a tidal bore, funnelled into the narrowing estuary of the Kent on high spring tides. A siren is sounded as a warning, but you can watch the natural phenomenon safely from Arnside's little pier, where this walk starts. Tide times are also displayed here and if you're intending to walk along the foreshore it's imperative that you check there is sufficient time at low water. Walk along the attractive promenade (some limited roadside parking) with its variety of gift shops bookended by the Albion Hotel at the corner. The road soon ends and a path continues alongside the Kent, signed for New Barns Bay.

After the coastguard station, the public footpath's course lies along the shore, which is a mixture of hard sand, stones and the occasional bit of concrete. The way is not difficult but be alert for high tides which may make it difficult or impossible to pass.

Approaching New Barns Bay, the path veers into the saltmarsh and reaches a concrete road. Turn right to reach the entrance to New Barns Caravan Park. Here, the walk turns left along the roadway and then continues along a waymarked public footpath through the pleasant secluded site, shrouded in oakwoods. At the far end of the site, bear left at a junction (SP Far Arnside). A narrow footpath now hugs the coastline on the top of low cliffs, sometimes diving into trees, at other times opening out to grand views across Morecambe Bay. Depending on the tide, the waves could be crashing against the cliffs at your feet or, alternatively, the vast sandy wilderness of the Bay may stretch as far as the eye can see.

Soon after a short rise, enter Far Arnside Caravan Park and follow the public footpath through the site onto the lane beyond. Shortly after leaving the site, turn left onto a footpath for Arnside via the Knott, running beside a field to Hollins Farm. Turn left, alongside the buildings, signed for Arnside, and go through a gate into open heathland. A grassy path rises through this National Trust-owned heathland, cloaked in bracken, brambles, hawthorn and oak. This is a thriving habitat for butterflies, with at least 34 out of the 59 UK species found on Arnside Knott. At the top, go through a gate and cross the bridleway, Saul's Drive, keeping straight ahead, signed for Arnside Knott. A steep stony path now negotiates the higher part of the Knott. As height is gained and views open out, bear left to take a path climbing around the edge of the Knott to reach the toposcope. Although this isn't the summit (which lies 500m east of here), it's the best viewpoint. A steep stony descent leads directly downhill towards the estuary but it soon returns to the track, Saul's Drive.

Turn right, cross a cattle grid and then use a field path parallel to the road, heading downhill. Entering Arnside, the road dips and then slightly rises. Just beyond, opposite a small postbox, bear left down a footpath (SP Promenade) to return to the start.

13

Warton Crag

Distance 4km **Time** 1 hour 30
Terrain rocky paths and grassy tracks
with some gentle clambering needed in
places **Map** OS Explorer OL7 **Access** buses
from Lancaster and Carnforth to Warton;
the railway station at Carnforth is about
2km away

The limestone hills around Carnforth,
Silverdale and Arnside provide an
exceptional habitat for a wide diversity of
plants, birdlife and butterflies at the
border of many northern and southern
species. Warton Crag includes no less
than four nature reserves protecting its
scars, cliffs, grasslands and woods. The
name Warton means 'Lookout' and the
crag commands a strategic position
alongside the narrow coastal route
north. The village of Warton was home to
the medieval ancestors of the first US
president, George Washington. On 4th
July the stars and stripes fly above the
parish church.

There's a small car park on Crag Road,
just off Main Street, in Warton village. The
nearby Old Rectory is an English Heritage
property open to the public. From the
back of the car park, a rocky path rises at
the base of an old quarry, coming to a gap
in the stone wall above.

Turn right, going through a wooden
gate, and then turn left, resuming the
climb through grasslands and alongside
a small scar hosting a rock garden of
limestone-loving plants such as thyme
and kidney vetch. As you gain height, the
views widen across Morecambe Bay. Soon
the path is high above the edge of a cliff
and a quarry below. Pass through a
kissing gate, then veer right to take a
grassy path rising directly towards the
top of the hill. Clamber up several scars,
not difficult but needing an occasional
hand. The area is a Site of Special
Scientific Interest with limestone
grassland, scrub and woodland providing
habitats for plants and birds such as

blackcap, marsh tit and bullfinch. Butterflies also abound, including the High Brown and Pearl-bordered fritillaries. Above the biggest scar, continue through hawthorn scrub to the top of the hill.

A metal beacon and a trig point mark the highest point with its expansive views across the Arnside and Silverdale Area of Outstanding Natural Beauty. The summit was probably the site of an ancient British fort, and artefacts from Neolithic and Roman periods have been found nearby. From the beacon, take the main path descending gradually through an area of cleared woodland studded with limestone boulders. At a walled bridleway, turn right to follow this attractive green lane around the flank of the hill.

Moss-covered walls border the route, dappled by the shade of mixed natural woodland. Bluebells, violets, primroses, wood anemones and celandine all take their turn at carpeting the route as the season progresses. Later, the track descends more steeply. As it approaches a road, about 50m before a house, watch out for a gap in the stone wall on the right, with a board indicating Warton Crag Nature Reserve.

Turn right through here to follow a woodland path ambling along the edge of the covert. After around 500m, you come to a kissing gate and join your outward route. Immediately after the gate, turn left through the gap in the wall and follow the path back down to the car park.

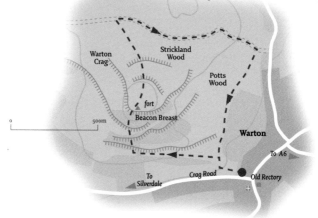

Lancaster, the Lune and the canal

Distance 16km **Time** 5 hours (can be shortened) **Terrain** riverside tracks and canal towpath; mostly straightforward and level **Map** OS Explorer OL41 **Access** trains and buses to Lancaster city centre

Lancaster's maritime history and strategic location on the main north-south routes have always given the city a significance far beyond its modest size. There is much to discover, such as the Maritime Museum, Castle, Priory Church and Williamson Park. This walk focuses on water, accompanying the Lune upstream to the photogenic gem of Crook o' Lune, returning across the historic Lune Aqueduct and along the Lancaster Canal.

Start from the Priory Church in the centre of Lancaster. Together with the castle, the church occupies a strategic position on a knoll overlooking the city with extensive views across Morecambe Bay and towards the mountainous profile of the Lake District. From the main entrance of the Priory, take the footpath heading north downhill, signposted for St George's Quay and Maritime Museum. The historic and strategic significance of this place is underlined by the remains of a Roman bathhouse a little way to the right of the path. A few more steps down bring the path to the course of an old railway line. Turn right to follow the track-bed, now a path and cycleway, soon viewing the Lune and the stylish Millennium footbridge as it crosses the river. Keep straight ahead but shortly spiral under the main road, staying on the route signed towards Caton.

The cycleway and footpath continue

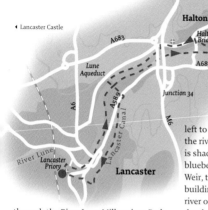

◄ Lancaster Castle

through the River Lune Millennium Park. Look out for birds and waders as the river is tidal at this point. The city is gradually left behind as the Lune Aqueduct appears ahead, carrying the Lancaster Canal across the river. Pass beneath this and continue along the picturesque wooded route, later passing under the noisy M6 motorway before reaching Halton Bridge, site of the old station (parking available here). Carry on through the countryside for a further 2km, then cross the river to reach Crook o'Lune, so named because of its sinuous course around an outcrop of hard rock here. A picnic site, toilets and car park lie just to the left, along with a refreshment hut and a lovely viewpoint.

From the viewpoint and picnic tables, a gate to the left leads onto the Tramper Trail which curves round a field with splendid views over the valley. On reaching the road, dogleg right and then left to take a footpath which descends to the riverbank. An attractive waterside path is shaded by beech trees and fringed with bluebells in season. Approaching Halton Weir, turn left down steps to pass some buildings and continue alongside the river on a track. Pass through a housing development until you come to a road adjacent to the narrow Halton Bridge.

Turn right here for a few metres, then turn left onto a busier road next to the Greyhound pub. Walk through the village, passing St Wilfrid's Church on the right. Immediately after going under the M6, turn left across a stile to follow a footpath which now takes to the riverbank. Straight after passing under the aqueduct, go right up a path and steps to reach the canal and towpath at the top.

From here, the route into Lancaster simply follows the towpath on an elevated contour above the city. At Bridge 102, leave the canal to go up the steps and then turn right down Moor Lane. Just after the Duke's Theatre, cross the main road and then walk up Church Street and through a pedestrianised area. Keep straight ahead across another main road to reach the Castle and Priory Church.

Kirkby Lonsdale and the Lune Valley

Distance 7km **Time** 2 hours
Terrain undulating route using field
paths and quiet lanes, returning along
the riverside **Map** OS Explorer OL2
Access buses to Kirkby Lonsdale from
Lancaster and Settle

The Lune Valley provides a tranquil
interlude between the uplands of the
Yorkshire Dales and the mountains of the
Lake District. At its heart lies the market
town of Kirkby Lonsdale. It is worth
exploring this town and the vantage
point of Ruskin's View, named after John
Ruskin, the Victorian art critic,
philosopher and philanthropist, who
lived in the neighbouring Lake District.
This walk explores the hinterland of the
town, visits the attractive village of
Whittington and ambles along the river.

Start from the ancient arches of Devil's
Bridge, crossing the River Lune on the
edge of Kirkby Lonsdale. The bridge may

date from the 12th century and is a
popular beauty spot. Parking is available
here and elsewhere in the town. These
days, the main road leaps across the river
on the modern bridge nearby. Between
the two crossings is the green shard of
Jubilee Park. To get going, cross the park
and picnic area to reach a kissing gate
onto the main road (the right-hand
option). Cross the A65 with due caution
and take the footpath opposite, over a
small field and between houses, to reach
another road. On the far side, find a
footpath signed for Wood End, leaving the
town and ascending a steep grassy bank.

The route levels off before contouring
along a grassy terrace above Kirkby
Lonsdale and next to a wood. To the
north rise the rounded fells of the
Howgills. Approaching the hamlet of
Low Biggins, watch for a gate in the wall
on the left, then cross a small paddock
and, just beyond a barn, come to a path

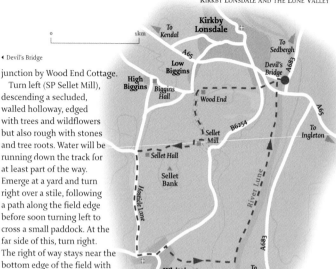

◀ Devil's Bridge

junction by Wood End Cottage.

Turn left (SP Sellet Mill), descending a secluded, walled holloway, edged with trees and wildflowers but also rough with stones and tree roots. Water will be running down the track for at least part of the way. Emerge at a yard and turn right over a stile, following a path along the field edge before soon turning left to cross a small paddock. At the far side of this, turn right. The right of way stays near the bottom edge of the field with the mound of Sellet Bank to the left. In around 500m, look out for a stile by a gap in the hedge on the right. The path now follows a fence bounding a small wood, steering round the buildings of Sellet Hall to come to a road junction. Turn left and walk along a very quiet and barely used road, Hosticle Lane, until you arrive at the village of Whittington.

The parish church of St Michael stands ahead, topping a small hill in common with many churches sharing its angelic dedication. Turn left and walk beside the road through the village, bearing left at a road junction towards Kirkby Lonsdale. Some 200m later, look for a footpath sign on the right. Follow the path through a series of fields, heading towards the distant profile of Ingleborough. Coming upon a track, bear left and use this route to arrive at a small dip, where the track forks. Bear left across the ditch and then take the hedged track to the river.

Turn left and follow the tranquil riverbank towards Kirkby Lonsdale. The riverbank is pockmarked with holes used by sand martins. Herons and mergansers are among the birds that inhabit the serene and stately river. The riverside path continues back to Devil's Bridge, first crossing the main road. Take some time to explore the town with its narrow ginnels like Salt Pie Lane, the parish church of St Mary and a collection of cafés and pubs.

19

Ease Gill Kirk and Leck Fell

Distance 10.5km **Time** 3 hours 30
Terrain initially good tracks, but later on
rough and narrow moorland paths with
two steeper sections; return on a quiet
lane **Map** OS Explorer OL2 **Access** buses
from Kirkby Lonsdale and Settle stop at
Cowan Bridge, 2km from the start

A final swathe of Lancashire stretches
north from the A65 to take in the wild
and remote upland of Leck Fell. Hidden
beneath the ground is an elaborate
network of caves, at 90km the longest
system in Britain. Evidence of this
underground realm is seen in the
potholes pitted across the moor and
especially in the gorge at Ease Gill Kirk.

To reach Leck, leave the A65 at Cowan
Bridge. There is a car park next to Leck
Church, with a donation box for
contributions. From here walk 100m back
to the road junction and turn right
towards Leck Fell. Opposite the driveway
to the school, turn left along a narrow
lane, descending into a valley. At the end
of the road, continue through a gate onto
a track which then crosses a sequence of
stone-walled fields to the soundtrack of
Leck Beck tumbling through a wooded
gully to the left. Immediately after
crossing a small beck, you come to a fork
in the track and bear left, then come to a
gate. Walk through a wood before
emerging into wilder upland country
where the peace is likely to be disturbed
only by the squawks of pheasants.

Until now the path has kept quite close
company with the beck but soon it veers
to the right, climbing up the side of the
valley through bracken, which can be
overgrown in high summer. Immediately
after the second stile, you meet a track.

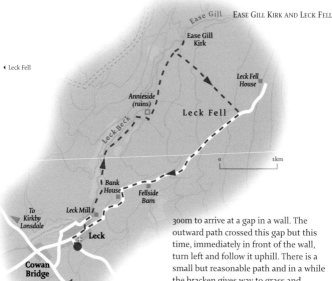

Turning left, the path soon levels out and passes the remains of the buildings at Annieside, now just marked by a lone sycamore tree. The way becomes narrower, little more than a sheep trod, and is soggy in places as it traverses rough pasture just above the valley floor.

Eventually you arrive above a fenced-off wooded gorge, close to the confluence of Ease Gill and Leck Beck. To explore, go through the pedestrian gate ahead and take the small paths up or down the side of the gorge. Although these are not unduly dangerous, care is needed as the terrain is quite slippery and steep.

Return to the gate and retrace your steps along the outward route for about 300m to arrive at a gap in a wall. The outward path crossed this gap but this time, immediately in front of the wall, turn left and follow it uphill. There is a small but reasonable path and in a while the bracken gives way to grass and limestone outcrops on a steeper section. Increasingly wide views open out behind, extending to the serrated profile of the Lake District fells and across the wide sands of Morecambe Bay. Above the rocks the path crosses heathery moorland, pockmarked by shakeholes and potholes. A little way from the path, on both sides, you can see fenced-off areas marking deeper and more extensive pots. Looming up ahead are the broad shoulders of Gragareth, crowned by its series of cairns posing as figures on the horizon.

Arriving at the quiet Leck Fell road, turn right to follow this back to Leck – you are unlikely to encounter much traffic as you enjoy the panoramic views ahead to the Forest of Bowland, the sea and the southern Lake District.

21

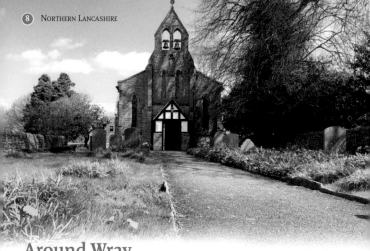

Around Wray

Distance 3km **Time** 1 hour
Terrain meadow paths and village
footpaths, almost entirely level
Map OS Explorer OL41 **Access** regular
buses from Lancaster and Kirkby Lonsdale

**This short walk around the environs
of Wray is full of interest. It crosses
riverside meadows, accompanies two
pretty watercourses and visits the
historic village devastated by a raging
flood half a century ago.**

There's a convenient lay-by on the edge
of the village, just before Meal Bank
Bridge carrying the road to Wennington
over the River Hindburn. At the far end of
the lay-by, take the footpath to the right
beside the river, soon passing a stone hut
with waterflow-measuring equipment.
The path weaves pleasantly across the
meadow while, on the opposite bank of

the Hindburn, the land rears steeply
from the water's edge as the river bends
towards the village.

Soon after the bend you pass the river's
confluence with the River Roeburn, which
drains much of the northern flank of the
Bowland Fells. This quiet river was the
source of huge destruction in the great
flood of August 1967 when nearly 5cm of
rain fell in just two hours and the water
rose 6m, destroying a farmhouse and 13
houses. Fortunately, no lives were lost.
Follow the paved promenade and path to
reach Wray Bridge, the original crossing
dating from 1780.

Turn left across the bridge and then
immediately sharp right along a tarmac
lane on the other side of the river. Pass
Wray Forest School and shortly after cross
a footbridge on the right, known as the
Kitten Bridge. The original bridge was

◀ Wray Parish Church

swept away in the 1967 flood and a more modern version now crosses the river. Just upstream is the site of Wray Mill, which operated from around 800 years ago until its closure in 1930. On the far side of the bridge a path known as The Spout accompanies the river through a charming wooded glade before rising up to a road next to the village primary school. Opposite, an imposing schoolhouse stands on the hillside.

Bear right along School Lane to reach a T-junction in the centre of the village. Turn left into Main Street, passing the parish church on the right and the George & Dragon on the left. At the end, turn left along Hornby Road, passing a former Quaker Meeting House. Wray had strong links with the Quaker movement and the meeting house was built in 1704. Just after the Methodist chapel, turn right into Lane Head, a public bridleway.

As you cross the riverside plain, you'll see Hornby Castle across the fields. The present building is largely Victorian but also incorporates parts of a medieval castle. Although it is a private house, the gardens are, on occasion, open to the public. To the east, the peaks of the Yorkshire Dales are ranged along the horizon with Ingleborough prominent.

Where the lane ends at a junction of tracks, keep ahead through a metal gate and along the edge of the field. After 200m, cross a pair of stiles in the hedge to the right to follow a footpath above the river. Cross a stile in the second field. Just in front of the wire fence beyond, turn right over a stile to take a narrow path between metal fences. Arriving at a track, turn left and then bear right. A greenway between hedges returns you to the start.

23

Sunderland Point and Sambo's Grave

Distance 4.5km **Time** 1 hour 30
Terrain track across saltmarsh, followed
by some rough terrain along the shore
before returning on a lane and bridleway.
Access around the point or across the
marsh may be difficult or impossible at
high tide. Fast-rising tides are a danger at
Morecambe Bay and tide tables should be
checked carefully **Map** OS Explorer 296
Access no regular bus service to the start

Sunderland Point guards the mouth of
the Lune as it drains the waters of the
Dales into Morecambe Bay. At low tide an
expanse of sand stretches almost to the
horizon, but as fast-rising tides engulf
the Bay the headland is the last outpost
of land on the Lancashire coast. The walk
explores the village, the headland and the
poignant memorial to a young slave.

  Start from Middleton Sands, reached by
road from Middleton village and Carr

Lane. There is a car park on the edge of
saltmarsh. From here take the track that
weaves across the edge of the saltmarsh,
basking in the vast seascape and views
that extend from the Lake District to
Fleetwood and inland to the Forest of
Bowland. You may spot the profile of Piel
Castle jutting above the sands near
Barrow or even, to the east, the flat top of
Yorkshire's Ingleborough. Here, pools and
gullies glisten while the trill cry of the
curlew resonates across the saltmarsh.
Where the track becomes a concrete ramp
leading to a gate, leave it and continue
along the bridleway, a grassy route
outside the fence and next to the
saltmarsh. After 1.5km come to a junction
of paths and a fingerpost. Keep straight
ahead here along the edge of the marsh.

  A short way further on you reach
Sambo's Grave in a small enclosure
through a gap on the left. Lancaster's

◄ Sambo's Grave

history is deeply embedded in the slave trade and 'Sambo' is thought to have been a servant or cabin boy transported from Africa to the West Indies and then to Sunderland, but the cause of his death is uncertain. In 1796, around 60 years after the boy's death, a retired schoolteacher, James Watson, installed a grave here and this lonely memorial is now a popular site of pilgrimage where tokens are left as a tribute to the slave boy and condemnation of the trade that brought him here.

Beyond the grave continue along the edge of the marsh, the route now needing more care across stones and rough ground. At high tide it may not be passable. Approaching the point, pass through a metal gate and continue along the shore, with the Lune emptying its water into the sea against the backcloth of the Bowland Hills while little egrets stab the sands at the water's edge. Pick up a path just before Sunderland Old Hall, and then walk along the track and lane past the isolated hamlet of Sunderland. The village enjoyed a period of prosperity as an 'outport' of Lancaster, used both for slave ships and for storing cotton, rum and tobacco from the colonies. When Glasson Dock opened in 1787, Sunderland became a holiday resort. Now it seems to be in a world of its

own, a small collection of houses reached by road along a tidal causeway. On approaching the second row of houses, turn left opposite a pillar topped by a stone ball. Follow a bridleway, The Lane, signed for Sambo's Grave. When the lane peters out, keep straight on along a walled path, crossing the neck of the peninsula to reach the western side close to the grave. Go through the gate and turn right, retracing the outward route but now with a vast panorama north towards the Lakeland fells.

Glasson Dock and Cockersand Abbey

Distance **8km** Time **2 hours 30**
Terrain **mostly flat along lanes, field paths and coastal embankment**
Map **OS Explorer 296** Access **bus from Lancaster to Knott End calls at Glasson**

Low-lying mossland spreads along the coastal plain between the Lune and Wyre Estuaries. Although close to the main north-south communication routes, this land is bleak and vulnerable, always at risk from the encroaching sea. The port of Glasson and the abbey at Cockersand bear witness to different aspects of history and life on these fringes. This walk leads from the busy dock at Glasson to the surprising charm of the inland mosses, as well as wide coastal seascapes.

Glasson Dock was designed to replace Lancaster as a port due to the difficulty in navigating the increasingly silted River Lune. A canal link was created, joining up with the main line of the Lancaster Canal a few miles inland. Ships still use the port today with more than 100,000 tonnes of cargo passing through annually, though it is also a popular leisure marina. Pay and display parking is available next to the lock and marina in Glasson.

Cross the lock by the roadbridge and walk up Tithebarn Hill. At the end of the houses the road bends to the left at a road junction. This slight elevation provides extensive views across the Lune Estuary to Morecambe Bay and the hills beyond. A toposcope identifies these surrounding features. Continue along the road until you reach a sharp left-hand bend. At this point, leave the road and keep straight ahead along Dobs Lane. Just before a bungalow at Kendal Hill bear left, bypassing the house. Just after crossing a small ditch in front of the yard, turn left along a track. When this dwindles out,

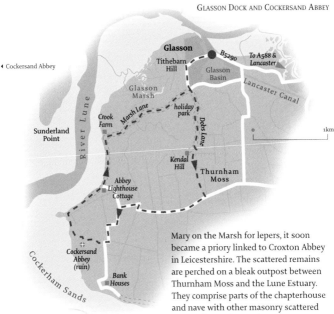

◄ Cockersand Abbey

continue straight ahead along the side of a field with a fence and ditch to your right. At the end of the field go through a gate and a paddock to reach a road.

Turn right and walk along the road for just over 1km, crossing the wide expanse of Thurnham Moss. At a T-junction turn left for Cockerham Sands. In a further 500m, on the fourth right-angled bend, the lane turns left. Here leave the road and carry straight on, going through a gate/stile onto a track. Pass to the right of a barn and derelict farm before reaching the site of Cockersand Abbey. Founded in the late 12th century as the Hospital of St

Mary on the Marsh for lepers, it soon became a priory linked to Croxton Abbey in Leicestershire. The scattered remains are perched on a bleak outpost between Thurnham Moss and the Lune Estuary. They comprise parts of the chapterhouse and nave with other masonry scattered among the grazing cattle.

From the ruins, aim for a stile a few metres ahead and join the coast path going north (to the right). This strides along an embankment which protects the flat and low-lying mosslands from the sea. A vast area of intertidal saltmarsh and sand stretches beyond the Lune Estuary. Pass Lighthouse Cottage, keeping ahead on a tarmac lane until you come to Crook Farm.

Here the coastal way turns inland to cross a series of fields, later passing a caravan site. At the road, turn left, retracing the outward route over Tithebarn Hill to Glasson.

The Forest of Bowland is a wedge of gritstone fells spreading west from the main Pennine chain, almost reaching the shores of Morecambe Bay. It is largely barren peat-clad moorland rising between the Ribble and Lune, penetrated by deep valleys and with little human habitation. The word 'forest' derives from its origins as a Norman hunting estate rather than the presence of woodland, of which there is little. Indeed, most of the land is still owned by the Crown and other aristocracy along with a water company. Before the introduction of Access Land in England in the early 21st century, most of Bowland was out of bounds apart from a handful of tracks and permissive paths.

Now the moors are open but Bowland's isolation is still real and its very attraction. You can walk for miles with little more than the cry of moorland birds and the croak of grouse for company. The landscape is in many ways more reminiscent of the Scottish Borders than the Pennines. Its remoteness has also contributed to its wonderful ecology, particularly birdlife. Hen harriers and peregrine falcons are here, along with many other moorland species.

No major roads cross Bowland, just a handful of more adventurous routes. The most famous is the Trough of Bowland between Dunsop Bridge and Lancaster, the road by which the so-called 'Pendle Witches' were taken from East Lancashire to the assizes in Lancaster Castle in the 17th century. Neither are there any towns, just a few attractive villages and hamlets, mostly around its fringe.

All this contributes to Bowland's spectacular value as a place to walk, from riverside rambles to moorland yomps. There is plenty to see and lots of space within which to see it.

Birk Bank, Clougha ▶

Forest of Bowland

Over Wyresdale

Distance 11km **Time** 3 hours 30
Terrain a combination of field paths and
upland tracks **Map** OS Explorer OL41
Access no regular public transport to
the start

The quiet estate village of Abbeystead
is set by the confluence of the Tarnbrook
and Marshaw Wyres. The two tributaries
rise in a broad grassy amphitheatre
surrounded by the highest fells of Bowland
before becoming the River Wyre. This walk
traverses both the lower grazing meadows
of Over Wyresdale and the remote heather-
clad flank of Ward's Stone rising to the
north. A lane between Tarnbrook and
Lower Lee shortens the walk by 6km and
avoids the higher moorland. Note that
dogs are not permitted on the fellside
between these two points.

Abbeystead is a gateway to the ancient
pass between the Wyre and Hodder Valleys,
known as the Trough of Bowland. Near

this tranquil hamlet is Abbeystead House,
built as a shooting lodge in 1886. The vast
estate of more than 70 sq km was bought
by a trust for the family of the Duke of
Westminster in 1980.

To the west of the village at the former
valvehouse is a plaque to remember the
sixteen men, women and children who
were killed as a result of a methane gas
explosion at an information evening in the
water pumping station in 1984.

Start by the primary school in the
middle of the village. Walk east, soon
crossing the Tarnbrook Wyre at Stoops
Bridge. Continue along the lane,
ascending a hill. Just after the top, where
the road bends to the left, keep straight
ahead onto a public footpath.

The right of way crosses a sequence of
fields where the stiles will guide you as
you aim for a farmhouse on the brow of
the hill ahead. When you come to a road,
cross over and take the driveway opposite,

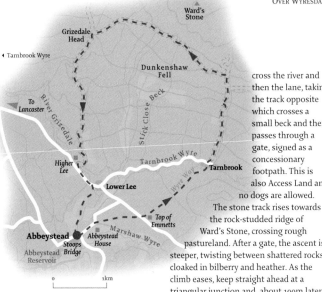

Ward's Stone

Grizedale Head

◄ Tarnbrook Wyre

Dunkenshaw Fell

River Grizedale

To Lancaster

Stick Close Beck

Tarnbrook Wyre

Higher Lee

Lower Lee

Wyre Way

Tarnbrook

Top of Emmetts

Abbeystead

Abbeystead House

Marshaw Wyre

Stoops Bridge

Abbeystead Reservoir

0   1km

cross the river and then the lane, taking the track opposite which crosses a small beck and then passes through a gate, signed as a concessionary footpath. This is also Access Land and no dogs are allowed.

The stone track rises towards the rock-studded ridge of Ward's Stone, crossing rough pastureland. After a gate, the ascent is steeper, twisting between shattered rocks cloaked in bilberry and heather. As the climb eases, keep straight ahead at a triangular junction and, about 100m later, bend sharp left, ignoring a spur going steeply uphill. The track now meanders across the side of Ward's Stone, below the ridge, but still with wide views, now across Morecambe Bay. In 3km, you arrive at a T-junction and turn left.

The track descends the hillside for about 3km, crossing moor and pasture to reach the road by Higher Lee. Turn left, walking along the road for about 350m. Just before a bridge, bear right onto a public footpath, crossing a stile onto a track. This lovely meandering trail leads you close to the beck through quiet meadows studded with hawthorn and gorse. At the end of the track, turn right along the lane back into Abbeystead.

signed as the Wyre Way to Tarnbrook. In 100m, in front of the building at Top of Emmetts, bear right across a stile to follow the right of way as it negotiates several grazing paddocks against the dramatic backdrop of the Bowland fells. The haunting trill of curlew, the whistle of oystercatchers and the 'peewit' call of lapwings pierce the silence of these bleak and atmospheric hills. The occasional enigmatic stone marker indicates the route of the Wyre Way, which traces the river from its mouth near Fleetwood to its sources deep in the Forest of Bowland, where a loop circles the headwaters of the Marshaw and Tarnbrook Wyres.

Entering the small hamlet of Tarnbrook,

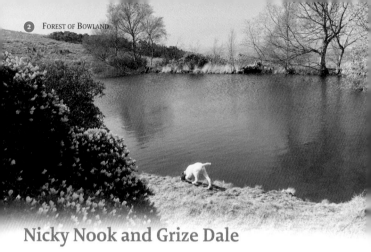

Nicky Nook and Grize Dale

Distance 6km **Time** 2 hours
Terrain surfaced tracks with one steep ascent to Nicky Nook and a steep descent into Grize Dale; some quiet road walking
Map OS Explorer OL41 **Access** nearest regular bus service from Preston and Lancaster runs along the nearby A6

The wooded cleft of Grize Dale burrows into the hills rising next to the M6 a few miles south of Lancaster Services. Within this small valley lies a small reservoir and a sylvan waterside trail while above it the summit of Nicky Nook has been a draw for generations of families out on weekend walks. At 215m, it is not particularly high but its position, protruding from the western edge of the Bowland Fells into the coastal plain, makes it a superb vantage point.

Scorton is an attractive village and a good starting point for venturing up the moorland fell of Nicky Nook. The spire of the parish church is a landmark for miles around, though the constant hum of the motorway detracts from its idyllic location. Start from the centre of the village, which has a shop, café and toilets. Walk up Snowhill Lane, passing the school and the Catholic church before crossing over the M6. Stay on the lane as it bends right by the entrance to Wyresdale Park and climb to a T-junction in the road, about 1km from the start.

Leave the road here, taking the footpath straight ahead through a wooden kissing gate to enter Nicky Nook Fell. A good stone path heads uphill amidst a sea of yellow gorse blooms in season: the ascent is alleviated by steps. As the gradient eases, pass a small reservoir on the right, before going through the kissing gate onto the moor. Down to the left lies The Tarn, a small reed-lined pond and a great habitat for birds and waders. Upland birds such as skylarks may hover overhead.

◀ Nicky Nook

The path continues steadily up to the ridge and onto the summit of Nicky Nook, marked by a trig point adorned with the red rose of Lancashire. The view is stunning and it is possible to see as far as the Isle of Man and the coast of North Wales on a very clear day.

Beyond the summit, continue along the stone path, reaching the edge of the moor before dropping into the deep wooded cleft of Grize Dale. Steps assist you down the steep hill but it can be slippery. At the bottom you come to a junction with a bridleway in front of a reservoir nestled in the wooded valley. Grize Dale means 'the Valley of the Pigs', possibly referring to the keeping of young pigs here, and there

are several valleys of the same name in North West England. Turn right here and enjoy a charming waterside track, shaded by a variety of trees. Beyond the dam, drop down among the sycamore and silver birch trees alongside the beck.

Further down, the valley begins to open out and arrives at a crossing of paths next to a footbridge. Turn right here, signed for Higher Lane, to cross a meadow, then skirt round the edge of Pedder's Wood in the shade of its beech trees. At the lane, turn right to pass the houses at Slean End. Immediately after these, leave the road to take a footpath to the left. Cross two fields to reach Tithe Barn Lane. Turn left and follow the road back into Scorton, going under the M6 on the way.

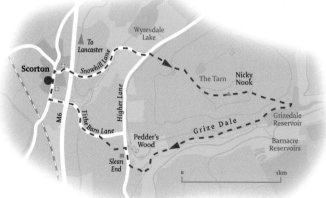

Clougha Pike and Grit Fell

Distance 11.5km **Time** 4 hours
Terrain narrow woodland paths lead to
exposed moorland with some rocky
sections; an excellent shooting track
provides a straightforward return;
sustained high-level paths and tracks
with superb views **Map** OS Explorer OL41
Access no public transport to the start

The Bowland Fells close in towards the
coast south of Lancaster, heralding
upland country which stretches all the
way to the Scottish border. Clougha Pike
looms over the narrow coastal plain,
overlooking Morecambe Bay and peering
at the distant peaks of Lakeland. Picking
a way through heath and woodland, this
walk loops around the moorland with
excellent views throughout. Careful
navigation is needed in places.

Birk Bank car park is on Rigg Lane,
about 1km north of Quernmore. To get
here, turn north off the Lancaster-Trough
of Bowland road at Quernmore
crossroads, then go right at a fork. A
broad track, in summer lined with
bilberries, leaves the back of the car park
and rises across heathland. In about
100m, fork right and soon turn right
again, descending into a wooded hollow
beneath a rocky crag. Turn left just in
front of a metal gate.

A narrow path crosses the marshy
hollow using duckboards. It then winds
uphill through an enchanted woodland of
twisted oak, rowan and birch trees where
a small beck cascades down a series of
rock steps. Emerging from the wood,
continue to climb a narrow stony path
through heather and bilberry to arrive
at a wall and two stiles.

Take the right-hand stile from which a
path leads uphill. Follow this for less than
50m and then watch carefully for a small

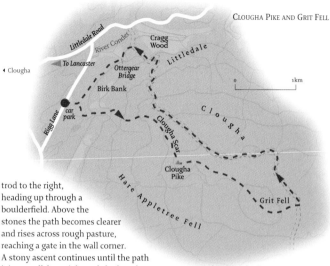

trod to the right, heading up through a boulderfield. Above the stones the path becomes clearer and rises across rough pasture, reaching a gate in the wall corner. A stony ascent continues until the path joins a wall; bear right and shadow the wall on your left. Go through a gap in the wall just beyond a gate and continue along the crest of the hill, eventually reaching the trig point. In clear weather, you are greeted with a magnificent panorama stretching across the Lake District, the Howgill Fells and the vast expanse of Morecambe Bay.

From the trig, turn left (east) along a footpath through heather. Cross a stile and veer ESE, later making a brief descent. About 200m to the left you can see a wide track running parallel to your route. If you wish to shorten the walk, a small path to the left links to the track, cutting about 3.5km (and a good hour) off the full circuit. For the main walk keep ahead until a stile and boundary stone indicate the slight swelling at the top of Grit Fell. Carry on past a cairn (the highest point) and cross

peaty moorland, gradually descending to meet an aggregate shooting track.

Turn left along this, ignoring side turnings. Just after dropping down and passing a grouse butt, stay on the main track as it curves left. The route leads close to a sequence of old quarry workings, still with extensive views, and then makes a steady but gentle descent. After a brief very steep section go through a gate at the bottom of a dry valley. In a further 350m the track comes to a stone wall at the boundary of Access Land. Immediately before the gateway, turn left along a track which contours above a birchwood, then crosses a dramatic defile at Ottergear Bridge. Beyond this a path weaves through delightful heathland, studded with boulders and colonised by rowan and birch trees, until you reach the car park and start of the walk.

Beacon Fell and the Brock

Distance **8km** Time **3 hours**
Terrain **field, woodland and riverside paths; the waterside stretches are sometimes stony with tree roots; one steep descent at the start of the walk**
Map **OS Explorer OL41** Access **no public transport to the start**

This walk begins at Beacon Fell, an outlier of the main Bowland massif. Clad in conifers, mixed woodland and heath, the hill rises to 266m and offers spectacular all-round views across the Lancashire plain and as far as Morecambe Bay. As the name suggests, its summit was a link in the chain of beacons used to warn of the arrival of the Spanish Armada in 1588. As a pleasing contrast, the Brock valley offers a tree-lined route beside a tumbling river, home to dippers, grey wagtails and kingfishers.

Park in the main car park at the Forest of Bowland Information Centre, well signposted from local roads. A clockwise one-way system operates on the road around the fell. There is a pay and display car park, and facilities include a café and toilets. From the car park, walk alongside the road going northwards. After about 300m, turn left onto a public footpath, heading downhill past the 'Life for a Life' memorial forest with sweeping views of the Lancashire plain as you drop down a steep field. At the bottom, dogleg right (onto a lane), then left onto White Lee Lane. This descends into the Brock valley, twisting over a couple of ravines before coming to Higher Brock Bridge.

Just before the bridge, turn right through the gateway, following the footpath to the left of the house, then cross a flat meadow adjacent to the river. The Brock tumbles through a defile colonised by ash, willow and alder trees and bordered by a range of wildflowers in summer. The path then hugs the riverside

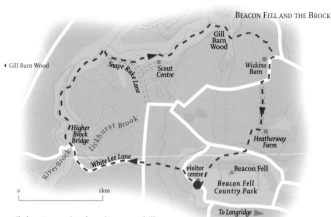

◀ Gill Barn Wood

until close to a weir, where it veers uphill, leaving the water behind. Meeting a track, turn left and follow this back downhill, passing to the right of a house.

Keep ahead along the valley floor, rejoining the river and its chorus of birds in the canopy above. Duckboards aid passage through a narrow gorge. Arriving at a junction, turn right, leaving the riverbank and following a stony track, Snape Rake Lane. At the top of the rise, it becomes surfaced and levels out. Watch out for a bridleway on the left-hand side (easily missed). Descend through pleasant woodland but, when the track doubles back to the left, keep straight ahead on a narrow footpath, soon crossing a footbridge over a side clough. Follow the right of way through the grounds of Waddecar Scout Centre, which later on morphs into a driveway. At the end of the grounds, keep straight ahead across two more fields to arrive at a footbridge. Immediately before this, turn right, crossing a stile and trailing the side of the

beck through Gill Barn Wood. Climb the bank to emerge into a level area of rough grass, now with the handsome profile of Saddle Fell and Parlick on the horizon.

After a while, the footpath turns right and negotiates the boundary of Wickins Barn, possibly overgrown in places. Reaching a road, turn right. After about 400m, just after a right-hand bend, turn left along a farm track, heading for the forested slopes of Beacon Fell. Shortly after the gateway to Heatherway Farm, turn right and in another 100m turn left, following the yellow-topped posts up the field.

Cross the road at the top and on the far side take the forest footpath bearing left and slanting up the face of Beacon Fell. Keep straight ahead over the brow of the hill, admiring the wide views towards the Lakes and Bowland, with the immutable landmark of Blackpool Tower also visible. Once over the brow, it's just a stone's throw back to the car park.

37

Fair Snape Fell and Parlick Pike

Distance 13km Time 4 hours
Terrain approach on quiet lanes to
exposed high-level moorland; compass
needed in mist Map OS Explorer OL41
Access bus to Chipping from Preston via
Longridge and Whalley

The high fells of Bowland rise north of
the village of Chipping and stretch across
to the valleys of the Wyre and Lune to the
north. The area is one of the quietest and
least populated in Northern England,
with extensive tracts of heather, home to
a range of upland birds such as grouse,
meadow pipits and even hen harriers.
This walk explores the southern flank of
Bowland, visiting the enigmatic Paddy's
Pole on Fair Snape Fell and the viewpoint
of Parlick Pike.

Chipping offers a selection of cafés and
pubs and is an attractive start to the walk.
From the centre of the village, walk along

Church Raike, past the church. Shortly,
branch off to the right, following a side
lane downhill and past a converted mill.
The quiet lane wanders along the valley,
next to Chipping Brook, passing a cheese
factory. Rising out of the valley and
emerging from the trees, the Bowland Fells
come into view ahead. At a junction, keep
straight ahead along Twin Brooks Road.

About 700m after the junction, turn left
along a farm drive (public footpath)
towards Saddle End Farm. Go through the
farmyard onto a hill track beyond. This
fine route meanders uphill, soon reaching
the open fell where you may find curlews
and skylarks wheeling overhead as you
make the steady but moderate ascent.
About 2km after the farm the gradient
eases and the track crosses the top of a
gully to reach a gate. Beyond, a good hard-
core path rises gradually across the
heather-clad flank of the fell, avoiding
nearby peat hags. It arrives at a gate right
next to the highest point of Fair Snape

Fell, a barely noticeable swelling on the long broad ridge. Cross the stile and turn left, heading towards 'Paddy's Pole' and cairn, roughly 700m to the southwest. To take you there is now a much more squelchy moorland path which attempts to wriggle round the worst of the peat, not always successfully. You will need to use a compass if visibility is poor. Cross a stile and pass a pond before arriving at the cairn and trig point.

There seems to be no convincing reason for the name given to Paddy's Pole, but its name and atmospheric location has made it a target for local fell races. Although not quite the highest point on the fell it is generally celebrated as the summit, perched on the edge of the ridge with magnificent views. From here, turn sharp left (southeast) to take a clear path along the edge of the ridge, curving round to Parlick. Beyond the col, the most direct route lies on the right of the fence, quickly reaching the summit. Don't be startled by the silent shadows cast by gliders from a nearby club, soaring along the air currents formed by the rising land mass.

From the summit, bear slightly right, descending southwest next to the fence. After a steep section, join a contouring path coming around the hillside and follow this to the left through a gate in the fence. The path rakes down across the flank of the hill to reach its base at Fell Foot.

Instead of going onto the road, keep left, contouring just above the moorland fence. Aim for a gate in the fence about 300m from Fell Foot and shortly before a conifer copse. Leave the moorland by this gate, cross a stile and then follow the right of way, marked by posts, across the field. Cross a driveway, climb over a stile and continue on the public footpath, which bypasses the house at Wolfen Hall. Next to the house, turn right along its access road, later arriving at a road close to Chipping Brook. Turn left over the bridge and climb steeply uphill for a short while. At the top, turn right along Malt Kiln Brow and follow the outward route back to Chipping.

Hareden Fell and Fiendsdale

Distance 15km **Time** 5 hours
Terrain good paths and tracks along the valleys but exposed peat bog on the high-level sections where a compass and good navigation will be needed
Map OS Explorer OL41 **Access** no public transport to the start

This is archetypal Bowland where long isolated valleys penetrate the heart of the moorland fells. There is an evocative appeal and rugged beauty in the peace and loneliness. Hen harriers and peregrines make these hills their home but still need vigilance and protection, and the terrain is reminiscent of the Scottish Borders. The central section of this walk is across exposed and pathless moorland, frequently boggy. Good footwear and outdoor clothing are needed alongside confident navigation, especially in poor visibility.

There is a parking area alongside Langden Brook about 4km west of Dunsop Bridge on the Trough of Bowland road. From here walk along the waterworks access road to Langden for just under 100m. Turn left through a kissing gate and cross the footbridge over Langden Brook. On the far side, turn left and follow the concessionary footpath for about 1km to Hareden. Cross a stone bridge to reach the lane and turn right, walking through the small settlement alongside Hareden Brook. Pass the water intake works, one of six in the Forest of Bowland, supplying Preston and East Lancashire with drinking water.

An excellent track makes a gradual ascent up the valley, passing under the watchful eye of Scout Rock. Towards the head of the dale, a very steep section raises the track above the valley and onto the high-level heather plateau. The grouse

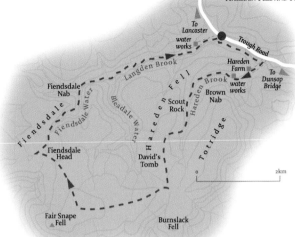

track ends abruptly. From here the route lies across open moorland and peat hags, surrounded by precious but treacherous sphagnum moss. The line is almost exactly due south and a series of grouse butts and posts aid navigation. Pass a shallow knoll, known mysteriously as David's Tomb, later reaching a fence.

Turn right (west) and follow the fenceline close to the top of a broad shoulder. It is tough going but gives a genuine sense of the wild country at the top of the fells. In about 2km, you reach a fence corner. Follow the fence round to the right for a few metres to reach a small cairn. At 520m, this is the highest point of Fair Snape Fell.

From here bear NNW, following the fenceline and an intermittent path, later veering northwest. In about 1.5km, a

welcome but all too brief section of flags bring you to a path junction at Fiendsdale Head. Turn right, going through a gate. Flags give way to a thin peaty path wandering across the heather-covered plateau. The peat hags soon coalesce into the head of Fiendsdale, dramatically incising the fellside. A narrow path traverses the rim of this deep defile, at first through heather and later across grass and bilberry. Beyond Fiendsdale Nab, it descends to the confluence of the Fiendsdale Water and Langden Brook in a wonderful amphitheatre in the hills.

Cross Langden Brook (care needed when it is in spate), turning right down the dale. Soon climb the left-hand bank to a shelf just above the valley floor and pick up a path with duckboards and posts to aid the route. Later, join a track and follow this for 2.5km back to the start.

The Heart of Bowland

Distance 16km **Time** 5 hours
Terrain upland paths, sometimes boggy,
contrasting with some quiet roadways
Map OS Explorer OL41 **Access** no public
transport to the start

This expedition entails a wonderful level
valley walk into Whitendale, a moorland
crossing into the adjacent Brennand
Valley and an inspiring climb up Ouster
Rake to the famous Trough of Bowland.
Though it's a long upland ramble with
some squelchy sections, it is definitely
one of the best introductions to the
Forest of Bowland. A direct track to
Brennand provides an optional shortcut.

Dunsop Bridge claims to be the village
closest to the geographical centre of the
UK. There is an excellent car park, with
toilets and even a boot-cleaning facility
found here. Start by the PuddleDucks
tearoom next to the bridge and take the
signposted public bridleway, passing a
children's play area and crossing some
open fields. A path continues beyond the
cottages and soon crosses the River
Dunsop by a footbridge. On the far side,
turn right and follow the tarmac drive up
the valley, an easy and delightful route
into the hills. The track is virtually traffic
free as it is a private access route for water
supply work. The upper tributaries of the
Hodder are the main source of water for
Blackburn. The terrain did not lend itself
to the construction of reservoirs, so water
is drawn directly from the rivers and
carried away via a system of aqueducts
and pipelines.

Just after a water company building,
around 3km beyond Dunsop Bridge, you
arrive at the confluence of two rivers. Cross
the first, the Brennand, and about 100m
further on swing left, heading initially into
the Brennand Valley. In another 300m turn
sharp right and rise around the edge of the
hill (though you can shorten the walk by
going straight on to Brennand). The track
follows the side of the hill for just about
2km before descending to cross the river
to arrive at Whitendale.

Map labels:
Whitendale Farm
Brennand River
Middle Knoll
Brennand Farm
Whin Fell
Trough of Bowland
To Lancaster
Ouster Rake
Beatrix Fell
Rams Clough
River Dunsop
Sykes Farm
Staple Oak Fell
Langden Brook
Hareden Farm
Hareden Brook
To Newton
Mellor Knoll
Dunsop Bridge
To Longridge

◀ Sykes by Trough of Bowland

0 — 2km

Look out for a footbridge on the left, signed for Brennand, and cross this. A steep grassy path later goes through a gate onto the moor. The gradient eases but the terrain is boggier as the route crosses the broad col between the Whitendale and Brennand Valleys. Coming to a wall, take the right-hand of two gates. The bridleway continues just to the right of the wall with no particularly easy or obvious pathway. In about 400m a short stretch of track leads to a gate, signed for Brennand. This improves on the other side and it soon bends right and descends to the valley floor. Cross the bridge and keep left towards the farmhouse. Here, turn right to pass the front of the house on a path bound for Ouster Rake.

Cross a stile, ascend a field and then go through a gate onto rough pasture. The faint path soon becomes more distinct and arrives at the fellside gate. The path beyond, Ouster Rake, slants up the side of the hill with views over Bowland. At the top, the vista takes in Pendle Hill and the distant sands of Morecambe Bay with the deep cleft of the Trough of Bowland in front. There is no obvious line across the inevitably boggy upper reaches but hold your course to soon pick up a faint path. In no time this loses height, increasingly steeply. After a gate cross a reedy pasture,

veering away from the small valley of Rams Clough and aiming for a little wood. A track takes over and leads through a gate down the hillside to the Trough of Bowland road.

Turn left along the road past Sykes Farm and then to the junction of the waterworks access road from Langden. There may be a tea wagon here! Turn right and briefly follow the access road before turning left to cross a bridge. A concessionary footpath now goes along the riverbank to the next valley, Hareden. Cross the beck and turn left onto the access road. Once back on the road, it's a 2km jaunt back into Dunsop Bridge.

43

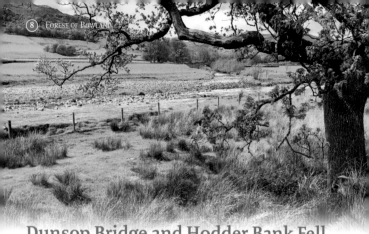

Dunsop Bridge and Hodder Bank Fell

Distance 7km **Time** 2 hours 30
Terrain riverside, moorland and field
paths **Map** OS Explorer OL41
Access no public transport to the start

The Hodder rises in the centre of
Bowland and weaves a route south for
nearly 40km to reach the Ribble. Once the
border between the two Roses counties,
its tranquil and picturesque course is
now entirely within Lancashire. The
water it brings from the high moorland
provides an important source of drinking
water for the urban areas around
Blackburn. This walk includes a range of
Bowland scenery: a riverside saunter,
open moorland and a final promenade
through Victorian parkland.

The Hodder and its tributaries drain
most of the Forest of Bowland with a
sequence of historic and charming
settlements along their banks. Dunsop
Bridge is surrounded by the Duchy of

Lancaster estate and sits close to the
confluence of the Hodder and two of its
substantial feeders, Langden Brook and
the River Dunsop. A stone bridge crosses
the water next to a lovely village green,
backed by bracken-clad fells and forest.
St Hubert's Church was designed by the
Victorian architect Edward Pugin. The
horse painted on the ceiling above the
altar is allegedly an image of Kettledrum,
the 1861 Derby winner.

From the car park, turn left and walk
along the road for about 100m. Bear right
between the gateposts to follow the
driveway towards Thorneyholme (public
footpath). Immediately after crossing the
river, turn right through a metal gate to
follow a footpath alongside the Hodder,
hunting ground of dippers and grey
wagtails who share the valley with a
variety of waders and moorland birds.
Stay alongside the river when the track
bears left to reach Lower Thorneyholme.

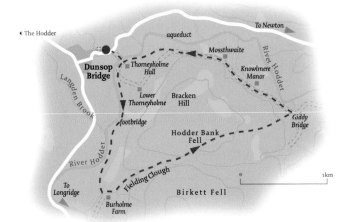

The path abandons the river when it bends away to the right and continues ahead across the fields. About 2km after leaving Dunsop Bridge, you arrive at a ford just before Burholme Farm.

Turn left before the ford and follow a footpath up a field and on into Access Land beyond. The path climbs the left-hand side of Fielding Clough, next to a fence. Alders populate the valley in contrast to the rougher upland terrain that has now replaced the pastoral setting of the Hodder riverside. At the head of the clough, continue over a stile. A good path now leads across the wide grassy dome of Hodder Bank Fell.

At the end of the open moorland, keep ahead down a sequence of fields to return to the Hodder Valley, reaching a driveway next to Giddy Bridge. Turn left to follow it

through the parkland of Knowlmere Manor on a concessionary footpath. The imposing façade of the 19th-century house lies to the right of the track. The manor dates from Norman times but the present house was probably built by descendants of Robert Peel, architect of the modern police force. Keep on the track until it ends at Mossthwaite and continue onto the concessionary path beyond. As Dunsop Bridge appears, you come to a gate and stile next to a signpost pointing back the way you've come. Climb the stile on the right and bear right to cross a field diagonally and find another stile close to the bottom left-hand corner. Head towards the houses at Thorneyholme, passing to the right of them to find a footpath alongside the river. Coming back to the driveway, turn right and return to Dunsop Bridge.

45

Gisburn Forest

Distance 5.5km **Time** 2 hours 30
Terrain forest tracks and paths with some
slight ascent **Map** OS Explorer OL41
Access no public transport to the start

Gisburn Forest cloaks a hilly region in
the far northeast corner of Lancashire,
just abutting the Yorkshire Dales. It was
originally created after the Second World
War and planted with conifers such as
spruce and larch. As these have matured,
they have been replaced with more native
broadleaf trees, improving the diversity
of habitats and the leisure experience.
Lapping at its foot is the 3km-long Stocks
Reservoir, fed by the River Hodder. The
forest contains mountain bike trails, as
well as a network of waymarked paths.
This walk is based on the Dale Head
Ramble, waymarked in orange.

Start at Stocks Reservoir car park on
School Lane, about 8km northeast of
Slaidburn. The car park is built on the site
of St James' Church which served the
scattered community of Stocks-in-
Bowland. Most of the buildings and homes
were abandoned for the creation of the 1.9-
hectare reservoir, completed in 1933. Stocks
Reservoir is an important site for a wide
range of waders such as redshank, snipe,
dunlin, godwit and turnstone, as well as
oystercatchers and curlew.

At the far end of the car park, go
through a gate and follow the orange Dale
Head Ramble markers. Several other trails
start from here, including one that does a
full circuit of the reservoir. Keep ahead on
the stone pathway, although you might
want to deviate left to the picnic area for a
grandstand view of the reservoir, or to

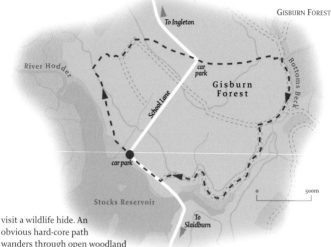

visit a wildlife hide. An obvious hard-core path wanders through open woodland with silver birch and willow, and the occasional patch of grassland sprinkled with wildflowers in summer attracting butterflies such as Painted Lady, Meadow Brown and Red Admiral.

After about 1km, turn right to leave the reservoir circuit path and gradually ascend through conifers next to a small beck. At a T-junction with a track, turn left. About 300m later, when the track makes a 90-degree right turn, look out for an orange trail waymark indicating a path leaving the track to the left and ascending a clearing with some felled trees. From here take time to enjoy views back across the Bowland Fells. The path levels out and comes to a road.

Cross this and go through a small car parking area opposite to find the waymarked footpath continuing beyond. Now narrower, the route penetrates dense woodland before descending steps to meet a track. Cross the track at a staggered junction, continuing on the slender path for another 100m to arrive at the floor of the valley in front of Bottoms Beck.

Turn right to take the path which trails just above the beck, adorned by vetch, ragged robin and clover. Native woodland such as alder, hawthorn and willow make an attractive backcloth. After 600m, where the main path bends to the left, watch out for a right-hand fork on a smaller path. This soon crosses a little wooden footbridge and climbs uphill alongside a very small tributary. At the top of the hill, turn left on a major track, dropping down through the woods to join another. Follow this, partly on the course of an old railway, to return to the road. Immediately before the road, watch out for a path going to the right which runs parallel to but segregated from the road. Later it swaps sides and returns to the car park at the start.

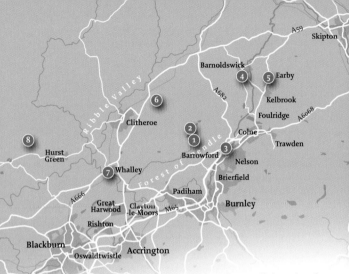

Pendle Hill is best known for its association with 'witches' but it has a much more fascinating history and landscape alongside its most famous tag. The mighty hill and its surroundings offer a compact and intriguing area for walking, with plenty of variety from fellside yomp to waterside idyll.

Pendle Hill is part of the Bowland Area of Outstanding Beauty, and deservedly so. The hill dominates the landscape for miles around, more because of its isolation, bulk and shape than its height. Although it is lower than the peaks of the nearby Yorkshire Dales, local people once believed it to be the highest hill in England. Certainly, the upper part of the hill consists of a vast sloping plateau of wild moorland and the views are magnificent.

For the walker, Pendle is not just about the hill itself. Around its flanks lie a chain of attractive villages, streams and woodlands which make for excellent walking. To the northeast lies West Craven, an area of pleasant pastoral scenery with the towns of Earby and Barnoldswick bisected by the Leeds and Liverpool Canal, the longest cut in the country built as a single canal. To the north, the Ribble Valley separates Pendle from the Bowland Fells. Here lie the market towns of Clitheroe and Whalley with deep historical associations recalled in castle and abbey. There are other hilltops to explore here too, from the slopes of Weets Hill, rising from Barnoldswick and almost appearing to ape its bigger neighbour, to the wooded height of Longridge Fell, the most southerly 'fell' in England.

Longridge Fell ▶

Pendle and the Ribble Valley

Barley and Pendle Hill

Distance 9km **Time** 3 hours
Terrain exposed moorland and a stony
descent **Map** OS Explorer OL41 **Access** bus
from Nelson to Clitheroe stops at Barley

Pendle's modest elevation, at 557m,
belies its geographical and historical
importance and the appeal it has held for
countless visitors. It is best known for its
links with the 'Pendle Witches' who were
convicted of murder and witchcraft at
Lancaster Assizes in 1612 during a period
of intense hysteria about pernicious
supernatural influences.

Later in the 17th century George Fox's
vision on the summit led to the
foundation of the Religious Society of
Friends, or Quakers. Pendle Hill
dominates the skyline of East Lancashire,
a huge whaleback ridge rising between
the Ribble and Calder Valleys. The
extensive moorland plateau is cleaved by
the deep trench of Ogden Clough and this

walk travels the whole length of this
intimate valley before rising to the
summit and enjoying extensive views
across much of Yorkshire and Lancashire.
Pendle is confusing in mist and exposed
in poor weather so be prepared.

Barley Picnic Site is an excellent starting
point, a grassy waterside meadow with
parking available. A refreshment cabin is
open most days. Barley's history dates
from the 13th century and its industries
have included agriculture, textiles and
cotton. Nearby farms have links to the
Pendle Witches and this history is part of
its tourist draw today.

Start from the crossroads adjacent to
the car park and go up the lane opposite,
along the right-hand side of the village
hall. Pass houses converted from former
waterboard buildings and then climb
uphill on the lane to reach Lower Ogden
Reservoir. Walk alongside the reservoir
and stay on the private roadway as far as

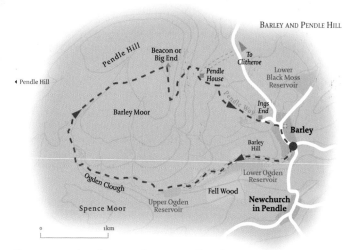

◄ Pendle Hill

the upper reservoir. Walls, trees and water add to the beauty and grandeur of the valley, one of the best ways to approach Pendle. Beyond the second reservoir, a rougher path now penetrates the wilder inner recesses of Ogden Clough.

Just after fording a small beck, the Pendle Way veers straight up the hillside to the right, taking a direct route to the summit. Ignore this and stay on the valley path, continuing just above its floor into the very heart of the hill. Later the path fords the beck, crossing to the left-hand side. There is a short sharp ascent before it trails along the rim of the clough. At the head of the clough, you emerge onto the sloping plateau which extends across the highest areas of the hill. Views now open out (mist permitting!) and a flagged path leads towards the summit. The trig point stands on the edge of the great escarpment that guards the 'Big End' of

Pendle, and views stretch across the Ribble Valley to the Forest of Bowland and over to the Three Peaks of Yorkshire.

From the trig point, turn sharp right (almost due south), following a path that gradually descends the moor and comes alongside the precipitous side of the hill. After about 500m, watch for a sharp turning to the left, a broad track that descends diagonally across the face of the hill, with lovely views to Barley and the Black Moss Reservoirs below.

At the bottom, some steps lead to a gate leaving the open fellside just above a farm. Immediately after the gate, bear right, taking the Pendle Way across a field above the farmhouse to a gate at the far side. An excellent, well-marked path now descends through pleasant meadows. Lower down, come to a tarmac driveway and follow this left for a short way before turning right across a footbridge to complete the last section into Barley.

Black Moss and the Sculpture Trail

Distance 6.5km **Time** 2 hours
Terrain hard-core tracks, lanes and field
paths; no steep hills except on the
Sculpture Trail loop **Map** OS Explorer OL21
Access bus from Nelson to Clitheroe
stops in Barley

**Nestling below Pendle Hill, Barley is
often the starting point for the ascent of
the mysterious whaleback ridge which
dominates the village. However, there are
many other enticing walks from here.
This one encircles the quiet slopes
around the Black Moss Reservoirs and
explores the enigmatic artworks of the
Pendle Sculpture Trail, hidden among
the trees of Aitken Wood.**

The car park in Barley (honesty box) has
a refreshment cabin and a pleasant
waterside picnic area. From here go
through the riverside park and onto the
road, passing the Pendle Inn. Walk through
the village until the road bends to the left.

At this point, keep straight ahead onto a
concessionary bridleway, signposted for
Blacko and the Black Moss Reservoirs.

This reservoir access road soon passes
the Lower Reservoir with the dramatic
backdrop of Pendle Hill looming behind.
At the far end of the first reservoir, turn
right at a T-junction and follow the track
round the dam wall to come alongside the
Upper Reservoir. About 100m past the dam
wall, turn right through a gate onto
a track for Aitken Wood and the Sculpture
Trail. It's a steep ascent but on a good
broad hard-core surface. At a junction just
past the steepest part of the hill, keep
straight ahead and begin the Sculpture
Trail, which does an anti-clockwise loop
around the wood, waymarked throughout.

Pendle Sculpture Trail features
sculptures in wood, steel and stone,
created by a group of artists who were
inspired by the story of ten Pendle women
tried for witchcraft in 1612. A local woman,

◀ Pendle Sculpture Trail

Alizon Device, was begging on a road near Colne when a pedlar refused her request for some pins. Following her curse, he dropped down dead. The local magistrate, Roger Nowell, investigated the incident and unearthed alleged witchcraft. There soon developed a frenzy of superstition and accusation, culminating in the arrest and trial of a dozen local women. The artworks include a unicorn, wolf and a life-size representation of the witchfinder. A tree sculpture recalls another local historical event in the 17th century when George Fox's vision on Pendle Hill marked the beginning of the Quaker movement.

The loop returns to the junction at the top of the steepest hill. Turn sharp right here to rejoin the main track, retracing your steps downhill to the perimeter of Upper Black Moss Reservoir. Turn right after the gate and continue alongside the reservoir. At the far end stay on the track until it comes to a road.

Turn left and follow the road, a very quiet lane with excellent views back across the reservoirs and ahead to Pendle Hill. After just over 1km, on a right-hand bend, watch out for a footpath going through a gate on the left. Take this path across rough pasture towards the reservoirs. At the end of the field, go through a gate and take the track beyond, passing a house and joining a tarmac access road.

Just before the reservoir, go through a gate on the right and take the public right of way, crossing fields just outside the reservoir boundary wall. The route winds down to the buildings at Overhouses. Immediately on the other side of the houses, after crossing a bridge, turn right through a gate, signposted for Barley. The path meanders alongside the stream on its return to the village.

Barrowford and the canal

**Distance 9.5km Time 3 hours 30
Terrain** **towpath, fields, a park and some
lane and pavement walking**
**Map OS Explorer OL21 Access buses from
Burnley and Higherford**

**Enjoy an interesting mooch around the
summit pound of the longest continuous
canal in the country, with a pair of parks
and reservoirs thrown in for good
measure. This is an easy walk with plenty
to see along the way.**

Pendle Heritage Centre in Barrowford is
an excellent starting point. The old manor
house at Park Hill is set in a park next to
Pendle Water and is now a visitor centre
and museum, with an 18th-century walled
garden and a fine café. There is parking
(charge) just over the road from the
Heritage Centre. At the far end of the car
park, look for a footpath running
alongside the Pendle Water. Reaching the
main road, turn right, passing the Old
Bridge Inn. Shortly, fork right along

Barnoldswick Road, then almost
immediately right into Francis Avenue.
When the road bends round to the left,
keep straight ahead on the footpath,
crossing a field after the end of the
houses. Head for the white lock keeper's
cottage and admire the views of the
hilltop town of Colne with Boulsworth
Hill as a backdrop.

Cross the footbridge next to the top
lock, then turn left along the canal
towpath, passing the cottage. As the canal
approaches the Foulridge Tunnel portal,
the main surfaced path rises to cross it.
Completed in 1796, the tunnel took five
years to build and is 1500m long. There is
no towpath, so boats were 'legged'
through by men lying on top of the craft
using their legs on the roof of the tunnel.
A track leads the short distance from the

tunnel portal to a lane. Turn left and almost immediately cross a stone stile to the right, taking a public footpath up the field to Slipper Hill Reservoir. Turn right and walk alongside the perimeter. Keep ahead after the end of the reservoir and at a track junction turn right. Pass Sand Hall and then the path of the former Colne-Skipton Railway before coming to a junction with a road. Keep ahead at the junction and bear left along a lane. Cross a footbridge next to the ford and ascend the hill to Colne Edge. At the T-junction, keep straight ahead through the gate, taking the path through Alkincoats Woodland, a local nature reserve. At a junction, bear right to stay on the public bridleway, emerging into Alkincoats Park. At the bottom end of the park, pass the car park and continue along Alkincoats Road.

At the end turn right to take the footpath alongside Barrowford Road. In 500m turn left into Ing Dene Close, then on a footpath beyond. Go down some steps and cross a very busy dual-carriageway with great care. On the far side follow the pavement around a pub and then cross the access road to Boundary Outlet. Take the footpath opposite, just to the right of the metal gates. Go past a group of houses to a road. Turn right and then immediately right

again onto the Route 68 cycleway. There is a pelican crossing over the final road and then a virtually traffic-free lane, Greenfield Road, continues on the opposite side. At the end, turn right to pass a terrace of houses and go around a bend. Just before walking under a roadbridge, bear left to take a ramp to the canal towpath.

Follow this left as it descends the flight of Barrowford Locks and crosses Swinden Aqueduct. Immediately after a 'changeline bridge' (where the towpath swaps sides of the canal), leave the cut and take the tarmac cycleway to the right, signposted for Barrowford Park and Pendle Heritage Centre. Pass playing fields and a velodrome, then cross the river and dive under the motorway. Turn right to follow the path through Barrowford Memorial Park back to Pendle Heritage Centre.

Weets Hill and Salterforth

Distance 11.5km **Time** 3 hours 30
Terrain firm tracks and paths with one
sustained ascent **Map** OS Explorer OL21
Access regular buses from Skipton,
Colne and Burnley

Although West Craven and Barnoldswick
are now in Lancashire, the area was part
of Yorkshire's West Riding until 1974 and
the emotional attachment remains.
'Barlick' is an interesting town,
straddling the summit pound of the
Leeds and Liverpool Canal. Its proud
industrial history includes the Bancroft
Mill Engine, as well as the more recent
Rolls Royce and Slumberland factories.
Weets Hill rises from the edge of the
town and provides an excellent
panorama and engaging
walk. A return passage
along the canal towpath
offers a contrasting
insight into this
appealing
border area.

There is a large public car park by the
supermarket in the centre of
Barnoldswick. The bus stop is opposite in
Station Road. From here walk through the
town centre along Station Road and
Church Street, then bear right along
Walmsgate, continuing into Westgate and
Colne Road. Turn right onto Moorgate
Road, also signed to a public bridleway,
and leave the town behind. Where the
road ends keep ahead on the bridleway,
now a lane, which sweeps up the hill
around a double bend. Pass Higher
Standridge Farm and, about 100m further,
look out for a stile on the right,
waymarked as the Pendle Way. The
footpath leaves the lane here and
continues parallel to it, next to the
wall. A steady ascent
brings ever-widening
views back over
Barnoldswick and
across the
countryside of
West Craven.

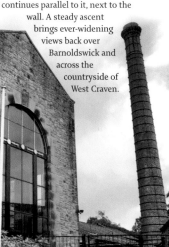

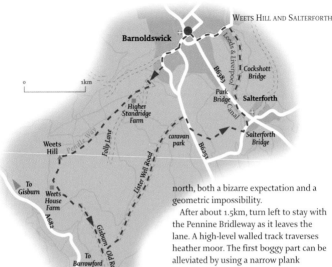

north, both a bizarre expectation and a geometric impossibility.

After about 1.5km, turn left to stay with the Pennine Bridleway as it leaves the lane. A high-level walled track traverses heather moor. The first boggy part can be alleviated by using a narrow plank walkway adjacent to the wall. It soon improves and eventually descends to meet a road. Turn right and walk along the road for 200m. Just after Knowlden House, bear left to take a field path slanting diagonally down the hillside. Descend several fields before the path becomes a track and then comes to another road.

Turn left to reach the Anchor Inn in Salterforth, here crossing the Leeds and Liverpool Canal. Once over the bridge, turn left through the car park and follow the towpath north. This is also long-distance Sustrans National Route 68, the Pennine Cycleway which travels from the Peak District to the Scottish border. Follow the towpath for 1.5km, going under the main road, past a marina and then skirting Barnoldswick. At Bridge 153, leave the towpath, turning left along Long Ing Lane back into the town.

Approaching the top, as the climb begins to ease, leave the wall and veer to the right, heading for a sturdy stone cairn. Soon after the cairn, you arrive at the trig point, marking the summit of Weets Hill.

From the top, bear left to rejoin the wall and shortly arrive at a junction with the Pennine Bridleway, next to Weets House Farm. Turn left through the gate along a walled track heading for Barnoldswick, which soon becomes a lane. It feels like being on top of the world with views across East Lancashire and way beyond. One of the sights is Blacko Tower, a folly capping a nearby hill. It was built by J Stansfield in 1890 who is said to have thought the top of the tower would capture views of the Ribble Valley to the

Earby and Pinhaw Beacon

Distance **11km** Time **3 hours 30**
Terrain **lanes, moorland and field paths
with a gradual ascent and descent**
Map **OS Explorer OL21** Access **buses
between Burnley, Colne and Skipton**

A gentle and steady ascent rises from the
pastoral surroundings of the border town
of Earby to the heather-clad moors and
wide skies of Pinhaw Beacon. From the
top take in views of Pendle and the
Yorkshire Dales, listening to the rasping
croak of the grouse or haunting cry of the
curlew. Enjoy the return by Elslack
Reservoir and through the charming
Dales village of Thornton-in-Craven.

Earby was once a major centre for lead-
mining and a small museum recalls this
history and its legacy. The walk starts

from the bus station, a one-shelter
turnaround bay at the head of town. From
here, head along Water Street, signed for
the hostel, soon bearing left and later
becoming Red Lion Street. Near the edge
of the town, opposite the Red Lion pub,
turn left onto a lane signed as a public
footpath. Almost immediately, turn right,
walking up the tarmac lane and away from
the town. A leisurely ascent offers
increasingly wide views back across Earby
and its surroundings. In just over 1km,
the lane turns off left to the final
dwelling. At this point, keep straight
ahead through a gate to follow a broad
track onto the moor.

The path rises steadily across the
heather, with one or two boggy dips, until
it reaches a metal gate where the Pennine

Way slinks in from the left. Continue for another 200m to arrive at a minor road. Walk alongside this to the top of the hill at a T-junction. You will return to this point, but first complete the conquest of Pinhaw Beacon by going straight ahead at the junction and staying on the Pennine Way as it uses a moorland track to wind its way to the summit and trig point. At 388m, the beacon commands an excellent vantage point as it is the last outpost of the gritstone South Pennines. As its name suggests, this was once part of a chain of communication beacons used to warn of danger during the Napoleonic Wars and other periods of conflict.

From the summit, return to the road. Turn right for a few metres to the car park, then go left onto a public footpath. A clear path descends through heather, reaching a gate and then going alongside a wall to come to a stile. Over this, continue to descend through cleared woodland to arrive at a track just above a row of conifers and Elslack Reservoir. Turn left along the track and keep ahead as it becomes a path and leaves the wood. Pass above Cooper House, cross a road and keep ahead on a farm track. The route goes just above Wood House and then runs alongside a wall to a junction with the Pennine Way (no sign). Continue downhill just to the right of a deep clough to a gate in the bottom left-hand corner of the field. Beyond Brown House Farm, the access road leads to Thornton-in-Craven, passing the abandoned embankment of the Skipton-Colne Railway, closed in 1970.

At the main road, turn left and walk through the village until you are over the top of the hill and heading back towards Earby. Then leave the roadside to bear left across a stile next to a gate. Take the track dropping down the field diagonally and continue in the same direction across a series of fields. After a small spur, descend slightly to join the track bed of the railway. This is now a footpath and cycleway leading back into Earby.

◀ Pinhaw Beacon

Pendle Hill from Downham

Distance 10km **Time** 3 hours 30
Terrain paths and tracks through fields
and across exposed high-level moorland;
a steep ascent and descent
Map OS Explorer OL41 **Access** bus from
Nelson and Clitheroe

A wild and wonderful alternative to the
well-trodden tourist route up the south
side of Pendle Hill. Although the walk
follows distinct paths, you are unlikely
to meet many fellow travellers as you
explore the northern side of this iconic
hillside. Starting from the attractive
village of Downham, the route also visits
the lonely watering hole of Fox's Well.
Pendle can be challenging in poor
conditions so ensure you have
appropriate clothing and can use a map
and compass.

Downham makes a fine start to this
walk up the northern flank of Pendle Hill.
There is a useful car park, complete with
toilets and an information hut, on the
southern fringe of the village. From here
take a track, signed as a public footpath,
bearing right off the lane to the car park.
This soon goes through a gate between
two houses, reaching a path beyond. The
first section of the walk crosses a series of
fields with gentle gradients and the
mighty profile of Pendle on the left. The
hill on the right is Worsaw Hill, a
limestone reef knoll, a geological contrast
to the millstone grit that overlies most of
the Pendle area. Clip the edge of the hill
at Worsaw End, then just before coming
to the buildings at Worsaw End House go
through a gate on the left. The right of
way cuts across a field and joins the
farm's driveway which leads to a lane.

Turn right along the lane, soon bending
to the left. Further on, where it switches
back to the right, carry straight on along a
tarmac track marked as a cul-de-sac for
Moorside Farm. Continue ahead when the
track becomes a footpath, eventually
arriving on the moor. Follow the waymark

◂ Downham

to the right of the ravine, with a steep climb to a marshy shoulder. The guide posts bear right across the shoulder and then lead the path steadily up the side of Pendle. The payback is an expanding vista across Clitheroe and the Forest of Bowland.

Towards the top of the slope, the path rounds to the left, now rising to gain the extensive sloping plateau that caps Pendle Hill. But it's still a way to the summit as you pass an imposing stone cairn built to commemorate the Scouting movement. Further on, after a stile, bear right and continue on the path steadily ascending across the moorland plateau to reach a gateway. From here, turn right and it's a short leg to reach the summit and the trig point that crowns it.

From the summit, retrace your steps back to the last gate. Instead of going through it, bear right. This is the top of the main path down the gable, or 'Big End', of Pendle. But, after 100m where the path turns sharply right to descend steps towards Barley, turn left over a stile. A narrow and exposed path now follows the edge of the hill before gradually descending across its flank. Part of the way along the path, notice a small spring

to the left, now covered by a metal lid and known as Fox's Well. George Fox is said to have drunk from the well on the day he climbed Pendle and had a vision of 'a great people to be gathered'. This inspiration led to the foundation of the Religious Society of Friends (Quakers). Lower down, the trod sidles into a bigger path which then zigzags downhill, eventually meeting the Barley to Downham road.

Cross the road and go through the gate opposite (SP Downham). Descend a few steps into a gully and turn left, then very shortly right across a stile with a barn on your left. A clear waymarked path descends a series of fields, soon joining a small beck to return to Downham.

Whalley Nab and the River Calder

Distance 9km **Time** 3 hours
Terrain field and woodland paths, with
riverside meadows **Map** OS Explorer 287
Access train service from Manchester and
Clitheroe and regular buses from
Blackburn, Burnley and Clitheroe

**Whalley straddles the River Calder in
a pleasant wooded valley. This walk arcs
around the town's hinterland, visiting
the landscaped grounds of Read Hall,
wandering alongside a peaceful stretch
of the river and discovering the wooded
knoll of Whalley Nab which overlooks
the town. Take time to visit Whalley's
most distinctive feature, its fine
Cistercian abbey, whose ruins date from
1330 and are set alongside the riverbank.
Its tearoom and picnic area provide
additional temptation.**

From the river bridge in Whalley, walk
north along King St through the town,
coming to a mini-roundabout at the

junction of King St and Station Road by
the Old Grammar School Community
Centre. Turn right along Brooke's Lane. In
about 200m, as the houses begin to peter
out, bear right along a track. Leave the
town behind, gradually rising alongside a
ditch until the track comes to a five-barred
gate. At this point, bear right and climb
along the left-hand side of an open
meadow, just above a small wooded
valley. Curve round to the top and look for
a stile on the left. Cross this and, after a
small patch of woodland, reach the
Whalley bypass near some traffic lights.
Cross this busy road to come to Spring
Wood Picnic Site.

Go over a stile next to the entrance,
marked as a concessionary footpath. Walk
up the left-hand edge of the golf course.
In about 300m watch out for a yellow
waymark, with the path leaving the
course and crossing a small area
of woodland. Continue

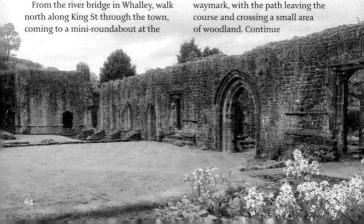

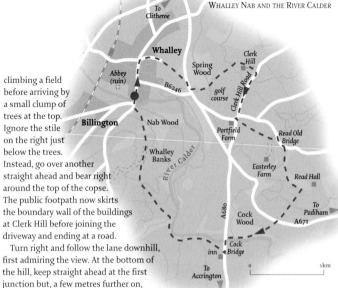

climbing a field before arriving by a small clump of trees at the top. Ignore the stile on the right just below the trees. Instead, go over another straight ahead and bear right around the top of the copse. The public footpath now skirts the boundary wall of the buildings at Clerk Hill before joining the driveway and ending at a road.

Turn right and follow the lane downhill, first admiring the view. At the bottom of the hill, keep straight ahead at the first junction but, a few metres further on, leave the lane opposite a cottage and turn left across a stile. The right of way crosses a sequence of fields, going from stile to stile. Pendle Hill frames the horizon to the left. Turn left on the track from Easterley Farm and come to a road. Turn right and cross Sabden Brook on Read Old Bridge. On the far side, bear right through an iron gate to take a track through the landscaped grounds of Read Park. The estate was acquired by the Nowell family following the dissolution of the monasteries under Henry VIII. Less than a century later, descendant Roger Nowell was the magistrate who sent the Pendle Witches to trial at Lancaster Castle in 1612. Coming to the tarmac driveway, turn right and follow this to the main road.

Take the track on the opposite side of the road, descending beside Cock Wood before passing a garden centre (complete with convenient café!). At the end cross the A680 and turn left, leaping over the River Calder on Cock Bridge. Just before the first house on the right, turn right through a kissing gate onto a path headed for Whalley Nab. Follow the path alongside and above the river to the hamlet of Whalley Banks. When the road peters out keep straight ahead, passing a farm. Soon afterwards, bear right to leave the drive and drop down along a bridleway with views across Whalley. At the bottom, cross the bridge and you're soon back in town.

◀ Whalley Abbey

Longridge Fell

Distance 4.5km **Time** 1 hour 30
Terrain moorland and forest paths, may
be wet in places **Map** OS Explorer OL41
Access no public transport to the start

Billed as the most southerly 'Fell' in
England, Longridge rises on the
southern fringe of the Forest of Bowland,
overlooking the Ribble Valley. Much of
the fell is cloaked in conifer plantations
of sitka spruce, larch and pine, with
native trees such as hawthorn and oak
also present. Despite this there are large
swathes of moorland and plenty of
open views.

   This short forest and moor walk reaches
the highest point on Spire Hill, with views
of the Fylde Plain to the west and the
Yorkshire Dales to the east. If luck is on
your side, you may even glimpse
Snowdonia, the Lakes and the Isle of Man.

   A minor road between Chipping and
Ribchester climbs over the flank of
Longridge Fell about 5km northeast of
Longridge. There is a car park just below
the highest point at Jeffrey Hill. A Roman
road is believed to have crossed the fell
close to here. Oliver Cromwell also passed
nearby on his way to the Battle of Preston
in the 17th-century Civil War.

   The start is itself a fine vantage point,
so enjoy the view before setting out on
a concessionary footpath, leaving the
car park and heading northeast. Cross

rushy grassland and ascend the slope gradually, with the Bowland range dominating the northern skyline. At a stone post, fork left and continue across the moor. Just over 1km from the start, you come to a stone wall on the brow of the ridge. Turn left and walk along the path beside the wall, with a plantation on the opposite side. The path steadily rises to the 350m-high summit of the fell at Spire Hill, topped with a trig point. Among the Yorkshire peaks visible from the top are both Ingleborough and Pen-y-ghent.

From the summit, retrace your steps for about 300m. Then turn left through a metal kissing gate. Immediately afterwards, fork right off the main track to take a public footpath which meanders down through the plantation. Emerging from the wood, arrive at a wall and turn right in front of this to take a path round the lower edge of the plantation with views towards the Ribble Valley. The path leads through bilberry and heather as it curves round the trees to bring you back to the point where the outward route first met the wall.

Cross a stone stile and turn left, following the wall for just under 1km until you come to the road. Turn right and walk along the road, over the brow of the hill and back to Jeffrey Hill car park.

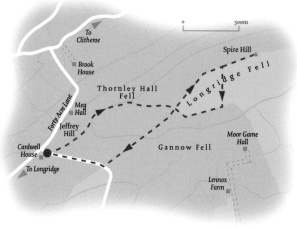

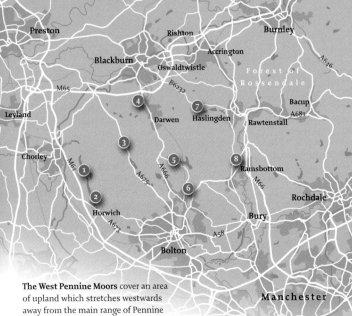

The West Pennine Moors cover an area of upland which stretches westwards away from the main range of Pennine hills. This arc of open country is easily accessible from nearby towns like Bolton and Blackburn and offers a sense of freedom and range of recreation opportunities long cherished by those who live here.

The Moors are designated as an Area of Outstanding Natural Beauty with a myriad excellent paths covering its 230 sq km. A large tranche of the area is also a Site of Special Scientific Interest, recognising the significance of the moorland and woodland which provide habitats for a variety of birds, including snipe, merlin and curlew. Its proximity to urban areas has also led to many reservoirs being built here. These bodies of water are of great importance to breeding birds, as well as lending an austere beauty to the landscape.

The walks in this chapter make the most of the moors and reservoirs but also include some surprising highlights, such as the remarkable landscaped gardens at Rivington and the enigmatic Jubilee Tower above Darwen. The area's industrial heritage, as well as its natural topography and well-maintained paths, all combine to make this great walking country.

West Pennine Moors

Anglezarke and Lead Mines Clough

Distance 6km **Time** 2 hours
Terrain good paths and tracks with some quiet road walking; a few short ascents
Map OS Explorer 287 **Access** no public transport to the start

Anglezarke Moor stretches down the lower slopes of the West Pennine Moors to meet a series of reservoirs built to supply Liverpool with water in the 19th century. Anglezarke Reservoir is the largest of these. Water is fed by the River Yarrow and other streams, including the beck flowing through the wonderful wooded recess of Lead Mines Clough. This short walk encompasses both the clough and the reservoir, enjoying the woods, moorland and water, with extensive views from the hillside above.

Anglezarke Reservoir car park is on Moor Lane, about 3km northeast of Adlington. From the road entrance at the bottom of the car park, walk east on Moor

Road for about 200m before coming to a sharp right-hand bend. At this junction, turn left, taking the side lane, Parson's Bullough Road, which rises through a copse to run alongside Yarrow Reservoir.

Where the road swings right to cross Alance Bridge, keep straight ahead through a gate to follow a bridleway into the delightful Lead Mines Clough. Lead was mined here on a small scale from at least the end of the 16th century, but ceased production in 1837. Many traces of this industrial activity remain, though limestone-loving plants have now reconquered the waste and birdsong fills the tree canopy. Walk alongside the tumbling cascades of Limestone Brook, bordered by wildflowers and grasses, to soon cross the stream. Pass a picturesque waterfall and shortly after bear left at a fork, soon crossing back over the water.

Immediately after the bridge, turn right through a wooden kissing gate. Follow

◀ Lead Mines Clough

the path along an embankment just above the beck, later passing the preserved pit of a former waterwheel. Double back to the left around the pit and ascend the hill diagonally and steeply. Shortly, zigzag back to the right to reach a memorial to a Wellington bomber which crashed onto the moors in November 1943, killing all six on board. Now you are out of the clough, the views open out to take in nearby Rivington Pike.

From the memorial, turn left and cross the next field to a gated stile. From here, a track leads across the hillside overlooking Anglezarke Reservoir and skirting the fringe of the moors above. Reaching a road, keep straight ahead, gradually descending from the moors towards the valley. The final section drops more steeply until it turns sharply right about 100m short of a bridge at the bottom. At this bend, leave the road and turn left through a kissing gate. A woodland path now climbs a bank above the reservoir and then negotiates a course along the edge of the trees. Cross some open fields before woodland resumes and eventually you reach a track

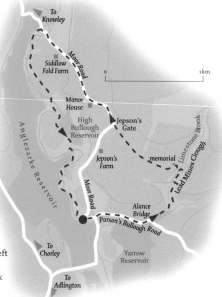

junction just below the embankment of High Bullough Reservoir.

Turn right here and continue on the main track to rise alongside the reservoir. A lovely walled track traces the edge of the water, surrounded by trees. At the far end, zigzag down to the larger Anglezarke Reservoir, continuing along a track beside the water. The track reaches the car park entrance, though there are also steps to the left before you get there, which cut off the corner and ascend directly to the car park itself.

69

Rivington Pike

Distance 7.5km Time 2 hours 30
Terrain level and well-surfaced paths in
the country park but steeper and stonier
tracks higher up around Rivington Pike
Map OS Explorer 287 Access nearest
regular buses in Horwich, 2km away

Early in the 20th century, William
Hesketh Lever fashioned the magnificent
Rivington Terraced Gardens. Becoming
Lord Leverhulme, William and his
brother James created the manufacturing
empire, Lever Brothers, best known for
Sunlight soap, though Leverhulme's
links with slavery in West Africa have
come to the fore more recently. This walk
explores the edge of the gardens, the
country park by the reservoir below and
the moors rising above to the landmarks
of Rivington Pike and the Pigeon Tower.

There are several possible start points
but by car the best is Great Barn
Information Centre where there's also a
café (car park closes in the evening). From
Great Barn, go down the wide track
towards the reservoir, passing the Go Ape
site. Turn left just beyond, following the
trail above the rope area and around a
small valley. Continue alongside and above
the lake, passing among mature beech
trees and winding through grassland.

At a fork in the path bear right to follow
the blue marker post, soon reaching the
'Castle', a stone folly originally built by
Leverhulme as a scale replica of Liverpool's
medieval castle. Though known as a
philanthropist who looked after his
workers at home, Leverhulme's palm oil

plantations in West Africa tried to enforce a system of slave labour long after Britain officially abolished slavery in its territories, and his firm's associations with a number of atrocities in the Belgian Congo are also part of his legacy.

Just past the folly, go down a path to the right to emerge at the shore and follow this left, curving round Crosse's Creek to join the main driveway. Turn right and walk along the drive to a car park.

Turn left along a path parallel to but segregated from the road for just a few metres. Then turn right, crossing the road to take the public bridleway along the side of the school grounds. Ascend to meet a wide track, turning right to enjoy a level walk as far as a metal gate. Here, double back sharp left to take a stone track rising diagonally. As it climbs it reduces to a gorse-flanked path.

Reaching a junction by a fingerpost, double back to the right, staying on the stone track. As you climb, the rounded moorland knoll of Rivington Pike with its crowning tower come into view. Turn right at a T-junction and, after 100m, turn left at a broad junction. The summit is reached by way of a stone track, then grassy path.

Go down the steps on the far side of the summit, soon meeting a track in front of a stone building. Turn right to follow the drive along the upper edge of the wooded parkland to reach the Rivington Pigeon Tower, built in 1910. From here you can descend the steps to explore part of the terraced gardens and an ornamental lake.

From the Pigeon Tower, fork left down a rocky track below a small copse. Eroded in places, this weaves down the hillside to a car park. Keep ahead on the tarmac road for a few metres, then go left along a level track, later coming to Rivington Hall Barn. Pass to the right of the hall and car park, forking left to curve around the bottom of the grounds before turning right to promenade down one of Rivington's broad avenues back to Great Barn.

Belmont and Spitlers Edge

Distance 13km Time 4 hours
Terrain excellent tracks with one wetter
moorland section descending from Great
Hill Map OS Explorer 287 Access bus from
Bolton to Belmont offers an alternative
start from Belmont village

The ridge of Spitlers Edge links Winter
Hill with the outpost of Great Hill and
offers an outstanding stride along the
westernmost elevation of the Moors. As
you might expect there are panoramic
views to the west and north, reaching as
far as the Lakes and Blackpool Tower.

Crookfield Road car park lies just off
the A675 Bolton to Preston Road, about
4km north of Belmont. Find it by turning
onto a minor road on the east side of the
main road, signed for Tockholes. Take the
path from the far end of the car park and
follow it parallel to the lane until it
rejoins this at a right-angled bend. Cross
the road, turning right onto a wide track

through a gate. An easy route crosses
rough pasture on the wide valley floor,
later passing Lower Pasture Barn Farm
before traversing the side of Catherine
Edge. Continue just above Belmont
Reservoir, home of a sailing club, as well
as one of the largest black-headed gull
colonies in England.

About 2.5km after the start, the track
reaches a junction just above the buildings
at Higher Pasture House. Turn right
through a gate here, heading for the farm
with the village of Belmont beyond. As
well as the Winter Hill masts, it is possible
to see as far as the high-rise buildings of
Manchester's city centre. Walk through the
farmyard, bearing left on the far side and
staying on the track which now descends
alongside Belmont Reservoir. Turn right to
cross the dam wall and, on the far side,
bear left onto a footpath slanting up to
join the main road.

Walk along the road for 300m, before

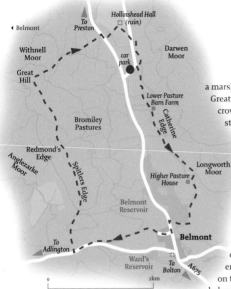

a marshy saddle before ascending Great Hill, its 381m summit crowned with a substantial stone wind shelter.

From here the main stone path bears west, but this route goes in the opposite direction, forsaking the hard surface and heading ENE to pick up a moorland path dropping downhill. This is not obvious at first and in mist you will need to navigate carefully, but once found it's clear enough. It aims for a house on the main road in the valley below, crossing some squidgy ground but with no serious difficulties. A wooden gate gives access to the main road. Cross the busy A675, following it to the right for 100m, before turning left at a public footpath sign. A refreshingly dry path runs through woodland and comes to a T-junction. Turn right to reach the ruins of Hollinshead Hall, all that is left of a large farmhouse built by John Hollinshead in 1776. Just above the hall, a wellhouse collects water which supplied the home. Continue on the path at the far end of the hall, rising up to meet a road. Cross over this and follow the concessionary bridleway through a gate on the far side. It weaves and curves above the road, before rejoining it close to the car park and starting point.

turning right into Naylor's Terrace. At the end go through a gate into a reedy enclosure. Beyond this, cross a stone stile onto the moor. Bear left onto a footpath ascending the side of the hill, with Winter Hill's masts brooding over the scene. Almost at the top of the hill, join a road and walk alongside it for 200m to reach the summit and district boundary. Turn right off the road here, the footpath soon crossing a wooden stile.

An excellent stone footpath now travels along a wide moorland ridge for about 4km, first crossing Spitlers Edge, then negotiating the broad breast of Redmond's Edge. Notice Darwen Tower to the east, protruding from its eponymous moor like a rocket ready for take-off. Cross

Darwen Moor and Sunnyhurst Wood

Distance 9km **Time** 3 hours
Terrain mostly firm moorland tracks and
woodland paths **Map** OS Explorer 287
Access no regular bus to the start but
frequent bus from Blackburn to Bolton
offers an alternative start from the A666
through Darwen

Darwen Moor is one of the most
extensive areas of heather moorland in
the West Pennines. Access to these
moors was won after an 18-year legal
battle at the end of the 19th century, a
good while before freedom was won
elsewhere in the Pennines. Stride out
over the moors to reach the
enigmatic Jubilee Tower before
exploring the woodlands of
Sunnyhurst Nature Reserve
and Tockholes Plantation.

Start at Roddlesworth
Information Centre, Tockholes
Road, Darwen BB3 0PA, about
8km south of Blackburn. There
is a café and toilets here, as
well as a nearby pub. An
alternative start could be made
from Sunnyhurst Wood
car park in Darwen.

Take the bridleway
going to the right of

Hollinshead Terrace onto Darwen Moor.
A good track rises across a couple of fields
and then becomes a fenced lane through
woodland. As the lane turns left to cross
the valley, keep straight ahead, through a
gate, on a path towards White Hill and
Great Hill. An attractive route ascends the
secluded valley of Stepback Brook,
passing a small but spectacular waterfall
cascading over a stone ledge. The valley
curves right and then left. Continue
climbing to the top of the groove and join
a bigger path by a small bench. Keep
straight ahead with views sweeping
across the wide expanse of the moor and
towards the Forest of Bowland to the
north. The Jubilee Tower lies to the
left, on the near horizon. In another
300m, just after a gatepost, take the
left fork, heading towards the tower.
An excellent sandstone path winds
through a magnificent stretch of
open moorland around the edge of
the hill until it arrives by the tower.

As its name suggests, the tower
was built to commemorate Queen
Victoria's Diamond Jubilee in 1897.
As this was only a year after
access to the moor was
achieved, it also came to
symbolise the freedom of

visitor centre

Darwen

inn

Sunnyhurst Wood

To Blackburn

Dean Lane

Roddlesworth Reservoirs

Earnsdale Reservoir

Sunnyhurst Hey Reservoir

Ryal Fold

inn

information centre

Stepback Brook

Jubilee Tower

Darwen Hill

Tockholes Road

Tockholes No 3 Plantation

To Bolton

waterfall

Darwen Moor

White Hill

0   1km

common people to enjoy the outdoors. From the trig point, take the track descending ahead, with the tower on your right. After a few metres, keep straight ahead at a crossing and continue downhill on the track, which later becomes a green lane as it leaves the moor. You come to the road at the Sunnyhurst pub.

Turn left and shortly after leave the road, turning right through the lychgate into Sunnyhurst Wood Nature Reserve. Descend steeply through the wood before arriving at the bottom of the valley and a junction of paths. The visitor centre and café lie 300m to the right but to stay on the walk turn left, signed for the Reservoir. An excellent woodland track rises gently alongside the beck. With luck you may see a kingfisher and you will certainly hear the calls of the woodland birds that make this peaceful valley their home. The track steepens as it leaves the woods and comes to the dam at Earnsdale Reservoir. Keep ahead on the bridleway for Tockholes, a rising green lane edged with holly trees.

On reaching the road, turn left for about 200m before turning right through a gate onto a concessionary bridleway in Tockholes Plantation. The first section may be muddy, but it very soon becomes a firm track, dropping through the woods with glimpses across Roddlesworth Reservoir. Keep ahead as a broader track sidles in from the right, and continue for another 1km. Just after crossing a small stream, turn left up a good track. There is no sign, but the junction is at the top of a short descent to a bridge over the river. If you get to the bridge, you've overshot by about 100m. Rise steadily, at first alongside the small stream among oak and silver birch trees. The path arrives at the road opposite the car park at Roddlesworth Information Centre.

◀ Jubilee Tower

Entwistle

Distance 6.5km **Time** 2 hours
Terrain tracks and lanes with one section
of moorland paths **Map** OS Explorer 287
Access trains to Entwistle Station from
Blackburn and Bolton

A series of reservoirs was built in the
19th century to dam the streams
emerging from the West Pennine Moors.
This pleasant and easy loop of Turton
and Entwistle Reservoir, lying in a
secluded hollow with trees to the water's
edge, contrasts with a higher-level return
across the edge of the moor with views
extending as far as the Peak District.

Start from Turton and Entwistle
Reservoir car park (BL7 0NH), reached
from the B6391 and set above the
southeastern corner of the reservoir. Make
your way down to the water's edge, next
to the end of the dam. When it was built
in 1832, this was the highest dam in

Britain. The wall rises over 30m from the
base and impounds up to 3.4m litres of
water. Take the sturdy footpath to the left
along the lakeside. This is a wide and level
route, with plenty of seats for relaxed
views across the water. You may spot a
cormorant, heron or great-crested grebe
among other birds. At the western end,
the reservoir narrows into a slender arm
and the path continues alongside the
stream. Ignore the first footbridge on the
right and keep going alongside a
sequence of shallow weirs to arrive by a
second footbridge on the right.

Cross the bridge. On the far side you can
choose a simple circuit of the reservoir by
turning right and following the northern
lake shore back to the dam and car park.
For this walk, however, turn left over a
stile, leaving the main track at a marker
for the Witton Weavers Way. Almost
immediately, turn right over a second stile

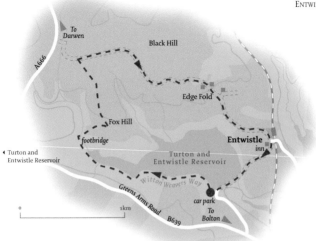

to climb up a field on a faint path weaving through gorse bushes. At a fence corner, it veers to the right and, in another 200m or so, comes to a junction with a grassy cart track. This section can be squelchy, so be prepared to pick your route across tufts of grass! Turn left and follow the track as it rises across rough pasture, now well clear of the trees. As you gain height, expansive views open out.

At the top, meet a good hard-core track crossing at a T-junction and turn right. Continue along this as it meanders across the hillside with a vantage south across distant Manchester to the Peak District beyond. Arriving above the houses at Edge Fold, cross a cattle grid and walk downhill. Keep straight ahead past the houses as the track becomes a sunken footpath. This emerges at a lane junction at the entrance to Delph House driveway.

Bear right and follow a pleasant lane downhill, with glimpses of the reservoir through the conifers to your right.

Reaching the hamlet of Entwistle, you also come to the Strawbury Duck. Yes, this is the right spelling, though there is no apparent explanation of its origin! The railway station is just down to the left here, a request stop on the line between Bolton and Blackburn. It makes a convenient alternative start and finish to the walk.

To continue with the main route, take Overshores Road, the unmade road going along the left-hand side of the Strawbury Duck. Pass the houses before descending to the reservoir. Keep straight ahead over the outflow and notice a colourful plaque marking the construction of the waterworks for Bolton. Continue over the dam to return to the car park.

Jumbles, Wayoh and Turton Tower

Distance 10.5km **Time** 3 hours 30
Terrain mostly well-surfaced paths, clear
to follow and with no steep climbs
Map OS Explorer 287 **Access** alternative
start from Entwistle Station with trains
from Blackburn and Bolton

The West Pennine Moors have been
a recreational green space for the
surrounding crowded mill towns since
Victorian times. The moors also provided
extensive gathering grounds for water
to supply local industry and people.
This walk visits three of these reservoirs,
as well as passing the evocative pile of
Turton Tower, a stately home for more
than 500 years.

Jumbles Country Park is reached from
the A676 between Bolton and
Ramsbottom. There is a large car park,
with a café, information centre and
toilets. From the information centre, head
north on the perimeter track running
alongside the reservoir. At the head of the
reservoir, keep straight ahead, passing a
footbridge on the left, now alongside the
tumbling waters of the Bradshaw Brook,
carving its way through a sylvan gorge.
Arriving at a housing development, turn
left over the bridge, waymarked as Witton
Weavers Way, along a cobbled lane.

At the main road, turn right, walking up
through the village of Edgworth until the
road bends to the right by the church. At
this point, turn left onto a footpath to the
left by the Black Bull, heading towards
Wayoh Reservoir. Just before the dam,
bear right up a concrete flight of steps to
take the perimeter path above the
reservoir for a while. Wayoh Reservoir is a
Biological Heritage Site and adjacent
Edgworth Quarries are managed as rare
traditional hay meadows. Continue along
the path with views across the water.

◀ Wayoh Reservoir

Further along, cross a road and keep going to the far end of the reservoir. Just beyond here, turn left to cross a footbridge over the river, still waymarked as the Witton Weavers Way. Shortly, cross a second footbridge and bear left, slanting up through the woods and leaving the reservoir behind. On reaching a road, turn right into Entwistle, crossing a railway bridge and reaching the Strawbury Duck pub. (The station is down the ramp to the right.)

Turn left in front of the Strawbury Duck, and walk along Overshores Road, really a track. It soon descends to Turton and Entwistle Reservoir and crosses the dam. Opposite the lower car park, take steps up to the right to the upper car park. Just before getting there, the track bends left, gently ascending through trees. Cross a road and keep straight ahead, signposted Witton Weavers Way. A lovely path weaves through birchwoods and soon strides out along the flank of the hillside, with views across the Bradshaw Valley to the distant Peel Tower above Ramsbottom. After around 2km come to a rough tarmac lane. Turn left, then cross an ornate castellated railway bridge, echoing the design of nearby Turton Tower. The tower and its grounds are to the left of the track and

easily accessed. Managed by Blackburn with Darwen Council, the grounds are open to the public while the house is usually open between the end of March and end of October (charge). It dates from the 15th century and includes collections of paintings and furniture. There is also a tearoom and shop.

On reaching the main road, turn left and walk along the footway for about 250m, before turning right along the signposted track. Pass an old pillbox, cross a field and then drop through woodland to the head of Jumbles Reservoir. Cross the bridge and turn right to follow the lakeside path back to Jumbles car park.

Haslingden Grane

Distance 9km **Time** 3 hours
Terrain paths through moorland and
fields, some muddy sections but few
steep climbs **Map** OS Explorer 287
Access bus between Haslingden and
Blackburn via Belthorn

For many years quarrying was a mainstay
of the Rossendale economy, employing
up to 3000 people. Today, it is still an
important industry, exploiting the
horizontal layers of sandstone and shales
evident in the quarry faces. Reservoirs
were built in the 19th century and much
of Haslingden Grane was flooded,
changing the face of the valley that had
once had 1500 residents. The area's wild
moors and relative remoteness also
made it a centre of illegal whisky stills.

There is a car park and café at Clough
Head on the B6232 between Haslingden

and Blackburn. To the left of the café,
find a gate and path leading up behind
the car park. After 200m of climbing up a
field, you come to a track crossing. Turn
right to join the Rossendale and West
Pennine Ways. Keep straight ahead at a
small copse and gawp down into the vast
chasm of Jamestone Quarry passed on
the right.

The path descends to negotiate the
defile of Deep Clough, crossing a
footbridge and passing a quarry lake
before the route swings left to divert
round another quarry. The moors are
dappled with isolated trees and echo to
the sound of the skylark. The path
becomes a track (muddy in places) as it
contours along Picker Hill. About 100m
before some metal barns, turn right (West
Pennine Way marker). Cross a stile and
two fields before passing Cloud Hill Farm.
A farm track leads beyond, with the whole
of Haslingden Grane valley at your feet.

Haslingden Moor

To Blackburn

Nab Hill

Rossendale Way

Deep Clough

Picker Hill

visitor centre

Jamestone Quarry

Cloud Hill Farm

B6232

Leys End

To Haslingden

Clough Head

ruin

Haslingden Grane

Calf Hey Reservoir

Ogden Reservoir

Holden Wood Reservoir

Musbury Heights

0   1km

Descend the track until you reach a second gate and cattle grid just before a right-hand bend near a house. Instead of following the track, go sharp right, crossing a couple of stiles and heading diagonally across the field to the buildings at Leys End. Pass through the farmyard to meet the main road.

Cross the road, being aware of the fast traffic at this point. On the opposite side find a stile and descend the field, aiming for the top end of Holden Wood Reservoir. Follow the path around the waterworks and across the head of the reservoir on a footbridge. A rather boggy path climbs the next couple of fields towards the mighty escarpment of Musbury Heights looming up ahead. Near the foot of an old quarry incline, turn right. A clear but rough footpath runs above Ogden and then Calf Hey Reservoirs before dropping to cross a deep clough at the far end of the latter stretch of water. Climb some steps on the far side and bear left, then stay on a good path now through conifer woods. Cross a

second clough in the woods, before curving round and dropping down a few steps to cross the intake of the reservoir.

Join a tarmac access road for just over 100m, then turn left past the ruins of Lower Ormerods. Originally built in the 1600s this was one of the grandest houses in the valley. The textile manufacturing Kenyon family lived and worked here in the 1800s. From here, a grass track weaves uphill. When it turns sharp left, watch out for a stile straight ahead. Cross this into a field and walk along the edge, next to a fence on your left. Near the top rejoin the holloway and shortly come to a T-junction. Veer left onto the track and follow this back to the main road.

You need to walk left for about 100m along the main road before crossing a stile on the opposite side of the road, joining the Rossendale Way. Climb a field to a stile in the top wall. Turn right, passing above a wood. At the next gate, turn right and return down the field to the car park.

Ramsbottom and the Peel Tower

Distance 8.5km **Time** 3 hours
Terrain initial steep ascent, then
moorland tracks with woodland and
riverside paths **Map** OS Explorer 287
Access regular buses to Ramsbottom
from surrounding towns

**The Peel Monument, commemorating
Victorian Prime Minister Robert Peel,
crowns Holcombe Moor and is a
landmark for miles around. A stiff initial
ascent out of Ramsbottom reaches the
tower, with wide-ranging views across
the North West. An atmospheric
moorland track, ancient woodland and a
riverside path complete a rewarding
circuit around the Irwell Valley.**

Ramsbottom sits astride the River Irwell
and the East Lancashire Steam Railway
and is famed for the World Black Pudding
Throwing Championships held annually
in September.

From Ramsbottom Market Place walk
up Carr Street, signed for the Peel Tower.
It's a steep hill as the road bends left into
Tanners Street, passing the sturdy, stone-
built houses overlooking the town. On
the brow of the hill, bear right up
Rawson's Rake, still climbing steeply but
later levelling out past the spire of
Emmanuel Church, Holcombe. The Peel
Tower now caps the horizon of the moor
just in front of you.

Just after the church, bear left into
Helmshore Road, passing the Shoulder of
Mutton pub. Straight afterwards, bear
right into Cross Lane. Where the tarmac
ends, bear right and take a walled track,
Moorbottom Road. In just 100m, double
back to the right on another track for the
final unremitting ascent onto Holcombe
Moor. As you reach the brow of the hill,
the track doubles back to the right, the
last few metres up to the Peel Tower. The

◀ Peel Tower

39m-high Peel Tower commemorates the life of Sir Robert Peel, born in Ramsbottom in 1848. Peel was twice Prime Minister and is credited with founding the Metropolitan Police.

From the tower, go north on the broad track running along the crest of the hill, enjoying the vantage points above the Irwell Valley and ahead into Rossendale. The track descends gradually, curving to the right to a track junction. Turn left and keep contouring along the hillside for the next 1.5km before passing the stone-buttressed barns at Chatterton Close. After another 300m, immediately before crossing a steep wooded defile, watch out for a stile on the right into Buckden Wood. A path goes downhill through the beechwoods, keeping close to the wall on the right, before emerging onto a road. Cross the road and a stile opposite, now descending a lovely wooded clough. The woods and much of the surrounding countryside are part of the National Trust Stubbins Estate, gifted to the National Trust in 1947 by Colonel Porritt in memory of his son Richard, killed in the Second World War.

Further down, cross a footbridge and stay on the left-hand side of the beck, later passing an impressive series of waterfalls. At the bottom of the clough,

wind through the houses of Strongstry, passing the embankment of a former railway, then ducking underneath a bridge carrying the present East Lancashire Heritage Railway. Immediately after the bridge turn right, following a public footpath alongside the River Irwell. Arriving at a main road, turn left and cross the river by the footbridge. Once over, cross the road and take the path to the right along the opposite side of the river. The riverside path continues along the valley before lurking along the back of a factory and through a small industrial estate. At the road, turn right to return to Ramsbottom town centre.

West of the Pennines, Lancashire slopes towards the sea, culminating in the coastal plains of West Lancashire and the Fylde. Much of this terrain is high-grade agricultural land and produces a wide range of crops. Ormskirk potatoes are particularly renowned. Part of the land has been reclaimed, notably the inland lake of Martin Mere near Southport, of which only a few remnants now survive. Walking offers wide skies and an abundance of birdlife. But Western Lancashire is not all flat. Ranges of low hills rise above the coastal plain, offering a contrasting landscape with wooded slopes and quiet streams. Among these are Ashurst's Beacon, the Clieves Hills and Parbold Hill.

Coastal Lancashire lacks rugged cliffs but has many other charms and dramatic surprises. The vast Ribble marshes provide a wetland habitat for many species of waders. The Sefton Coast, administratively in Merseyside, has one of the largest complexes of mature sand dunes in the country. Many of the coastal towns, such as Morecambe and pre-eminently Blackpool, were developed by the holiday trade and still express a brash sense of fun. Others have become more residential and retirement destinations or, as in the case of Fleetwood, maintained their maritime focus.

Five of the best walks are sampled here, covering everything from the Fylde Coast to the Sefton Dunes. They offer contrasting experiences of Lancashire's western seaboard and hinterland.

Western Lancashire

Lytham Promenade and Witch Wood

Distance 8km Time 2 hours 30
Terrain paved promenade, pavement and
woodland path, almost entirely level
Map OS Explorer 286 Access trains to
Lytham Station from Preston and
Blackpool South

Lytham's graceful promenade looks out
across the great expanse of the Ribble
Estuary. Its historic windmill bears
witness to the importance of natural
resources in the Fylde area of Lancashire.
A return through the local community's
Witch Wood completes an entrancing
circular walk, with the bonus of being
almost entirely level.

A convenient starting point is Lytham
Station on the South Fylde Line between
Preston and Blackpool South. From here,
walk along Ballam Road and on along
Park Street, through the attractive town
centre, until you reach the promenade
with the Ribble Estuary ahead. The view

will be very different depending on the
state of the tide. Lytham Green
promenade was built in the first half of
the 19th century, its main purpose as a sea
defence, but it soon became popular as a
leisure feature. Turn left and walk along
the promenade for about 500m to reach
Lytham Windmill.

The Windmill is open to the public
throughout the year, though the times
and days vary. It is also a lifeboat museum
and includes interesting displays on
various aspects of history. There was once
a series of windmills on the Fylde Coast.
Lytham's was built in 1805 and remained
as a working mill until fire destroyed its
mechanism in 1919. The old building next
door was formerly the lifeboat station,
but this has been replaced by the modern
base you passed on your way here. There
was a pier nearby as well, complete with a
floral hall and pavilion, but the whole
structure was demolished in 1960.

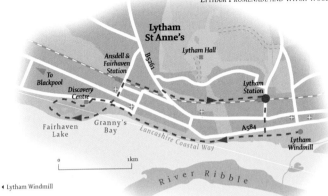

Lytham
St Anne's

Lytham Hall

Ansdell &
Fairhaven
Station

To
Blackpool

Discovery
Centre

Lytham
Station

Fairhaven
Lake

Granny's
Bay

Lancashire Coastal Way

A584

Lytham
Windmill

0   1km

River Ribble

◄ Lytham Windmill

Having explored the windmill and its environs, return west along the promenade, passing the modern lifeboat station and RNLI shop. Just beyond, the old mussel tanks site dates from the 1930s when mussels could be washed before sale and distribution.

Enjoy a saunter along the promenade for nearly 4km from the Windmill to Fairhaven Lake. The promenade is a flat tarmac cycleway and track with great views across the estuary. There is also an alternative lower path on the edge of the marshes. Fairhaven Lake was created in about 1890 when the new development of Fairhaven was being built. It is saltwater but only about 1m deep, so is a haven for wildlife and migrant birds. Walk around the seaward side of the lake to the far end and then return along the inland path. There is a café here and also the RSPB Discovery Centre which interprets the abundant birdlife of the Ribble Estuary. The site attracts more than a quarter of a million waders and waterbirds annually,

making it the most important single estuary for these birds in the UK.

From the Discovery Centre, walk the short distance back to the lake entrance, having now made a complete circuit of the water. Cross the main road and head inland along Marine Drive. Reaching the end of this short road, continue almost opposite into Woodlands Road, alongside the Methodist church, and soon cross the railway bridge over Ansdell and Fairhaven Station. Immediately on the far side of the bridge, turn right down some steps, taking you down to Oxford Road. Walk its length and then bend left into Bridge Road to come to another road. Almost opposite is a gate into Witch Wood. The path meanders through the narrow strip of woodland next to the railway line, originally part of Lytham Hall's grounds but then developed as a local amenity and cared for by the local community. In about 1.5km, the path emerges onto the road next to Lytham Station.

Ashurst's Beacon

Distance 9.5km **Time** 3 hours
Terrain field paths and lanes with gradual ascent and descent **Map** OS Explorer 285
Access trains from Manchester, Wigan and Southport stop at Parbold Station

Ashurst's Beacon presides over the Douglas Valley and the nearby 'new' town of Skelmersdale. The attractive wooded hill is capped by a stone tower, once a warning beacon for a potential French invasion. This circular route combines an enchanting stretch of the Leeds & Liverpool Canal with woodland paths.

From Parbold Station walk south along Station Road, soon crossing the Leeds & Liverpool Canal. On the far side of the bridge, turn left and walk along the towpath for nearly 2km. The houses soon retreat and the wooded flank of Parbold Hill rises on the opposite bank. At Bridge 40, leave the towpath, turning right onto a track over the River Douglas and then across a field next to a hedge.

After a short section on the valley bottom, the track ascends sycamore woodland carpeted with ransoms and bluebells in season. Arriving at a road next to Holland's House, turn left. In about 200m, opposite Lower House Farm, turn right onto a public footpath. The track ascends Ashurst's Beacon, first through oakwoods next to a deep ravine, then weaving between fields and woodland, revealing pretty views across the Douglas Valley. After a left-hand bend, the track levels out, contouring along the hillside to reach a lane opposite the entrance to Bangham's Farm. Turn right and walk up the lane past Ashleigh Farm. About 200m further on, watch out for a path in the hedge on the right, initially climbing a few steps cut into the red sandstone. The charming path contours

Parbold

To
Standish

Parbold
Hill

To
Burscough

A5209

Leeds & Liverpool Canal

River Douglas

◀ Ashurst's Beacon

Newburgh

0   1km

Prior's Wood
Farm

Prescott's
Farm

Holland's
House

Lees Lane

Lower House Farm

Hillock Lane

Higher Lane

Ashleigh
Farm

Bangham's
Farm

Ashurst's
Hall

Whalleys

Dalton

Beacon Lane

Ashurst's
Beacon

the hillside before crossing a sylvan dell on a footbridge. Continue across open grassland and another area of trees before emerging onto the summit of Ashurst's Beacon.

The area is now partly managed by Lancashire Wildlife Trust for its diverse flowers and grasses and is particularly valuable for various species of bees. The summit is adorned by a stone obelisk, built by Sir William Ashurst in 1793. Constructed at the time of Napoleonic paranoia, the tower was one of a chain of beacons stretching from Liverpool to Lancaster. A nearby toposcope celebrates the extensive view possible from the 170m summit, allegedly stretching from the Lake District to Jodrell Bank. It is a most attractive spot and a refreshing perspective on a wide swathe of the North West.

From the far right-hand corner of the tower, take a footpath heading downhill and northwest into a stand of stunted oak trees. The descent soon steepens to reach a gate. Beyond, the path leads between rows of hawthorn bushes to arrive at the grounds of Ashurst's Hall. The footpath takes you around the left of the grounds, passing a picturesque pond backed by Dalton Parish Church.

At the road, turn right and walk along the footway past the school. In about

800m, turn right along Hillock Lane. This quiet lane, bordered by hedgerows, ends at a T-junction where you turn right and, after 100m, turn left along a driveway through iron gates. Keep right at the fork, following the drive for another 150m, then going left through a gate to cross a field. On the far side, turn right onto the track, which turns left when it reaches the farm buildings. At its end, go over the stile and follow the right-hand edge of a field with a ditch to the right. Cross the River Douglas on a footbridge, walk through a meadow and a small hamlet to reach the canal at Bridge 39. Turn left to follow the towpath back to Parbold.

Rufford and Mere Sands Wood

Distance 8km **Time** 2 hours 30
Terrain well-surfaced paths, almost
entirely level **Map** OS Explorer 285
Access buses to Rufford village from
Preston, Ormskirk, Southport and
Chorley; trains between Preston and
Ormskirk call at Rufford Station

The largest freshwater lake in England
once submerged the flatlands between
Rufford and Southport. Finally drained in
the 19th century, the residual water is
now limited to Mere Sands Wood and
nearby Martin Mere, providing rare
habitats for birds and flowers alongside
the rich arable land of West Lancashire.
This walk starts at the nature reserve at
Mere Sands Wood, also exploring the
village of Rufford and the tranquil waters
of the Leeds & Liverpool Canal.

Mere Sands Wood comprises sandy
heaths, meres and wet meadows,
attracting a wide range of waterfowl such
as grebes and goosanders, with
woodpeckers and wildflowers found in
the woods. There is a visitor centre, toilets
and café, as well as the car park. The walk
can also be reached from Rufford village
(bus service) or Rufford Station.

From the car park, turn west towards
the Marshall Hide, taking the footpath
alongside the fence. As the path
approaches the edge of the reserve and
woodland, it bends to the left. At this
point, turn right onto a footpath signed
for Holmeswood Village, soon reaching a
road. Cross over and turn right, walking
along the footway for about 200m. At the
far side of the house, The Warren, turn left
along a tarmac drive which morphs into a

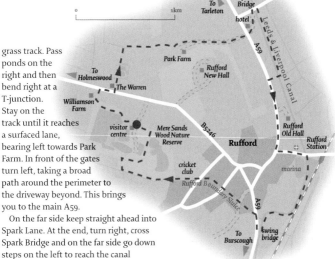

grass track. Pass ponds on the right and then bend right at a T-junction. Stay on the track until it reaches a surfaced lane, bearing left towards Park Farm. In front of the gates turn left, taking a broad path around the perimeter to the driveway beyond. This brings you to the main A59.

On the far side keep straight ahead into Spark Lane. At the end, turn right, cross Spark Bridge and on the far side go down steps on the left to reach the canal towpath. The Rufford branch of the Leeds & Liverpool Canal linked the main line of the waterway with the Ribble Estuary just to the north. Opened in 1816, the main canal was the longest single waterway in Great Britain; the Rufford branch was completed a few years later. Walk along the towpath to Swing Bridge 8, which you cross, and take the track to the A59. Turn left to reach the National Trust's Rufford Old Hall, a remarkable Tudor buidling that was home to the Hesketh family. From the hall, continue south along the A59 into Rufford village, then turn left to return to the canal. Turn right to rejoin the towpath as far as Bridge 6.

Cross the swing bridge. At the main road, go right for less than 100m, then turn left onto a public footpath just before a bridge. Follow a small waterway (Rufford Boundary Sluice), cross several minor roads and skirt some housing to come to the cricket club. Keep straight on, passing the pavilion and entering Mere Sands Wood.

Carry straight on around the perimeter of this pleasant mixed woodland, with the West Lancashire plain stretching away to the south. Stay on the main path as it curves to the right just before a barn. Cross a footbridge, then turn right at a T-junction, signed for the visitor centre. Just after another footbridge, turn left. At the far side of the wood, turn left at a path junction to return to the start.

◀ Rufford Old Hall

91

Clieves Hill

Distance 7km **Time** 2 hours
Terrain field paths and lanes
Map OS Explorer 285 **Access** bus from
Liverpool, Ormskirk and Skelmersdale;
frequent trains from Liverpool and
Ormskirk to Aughton Park Station, 1km
from the start

The West Lancashire plain stretches
from the Pennine foothills to the Irish
Sea and is some of the best farming land
in the country. Potatoes, onions, leeks,
cabbages and sprouts are among the
many crops grown here. The Clieves
Hills rise only about 50m above the flat
agrarian landscape. Among the
quiet lanes and field paths lie some
enchanting and secluded natural gems,
notably the Gorse Hill Nature Reserve
visited on this walk.

Christ Church Aughton crowns the low
sandstone ridge south of Ormskirk,
straddled by the A59. Because of its
position the lofty churchtower is visible
for many miles. Opposite the church, take
the lane signposted to Gorse Hill Service
Reservoir. In front of the water company
compound, turn left to leave the track,
following a footpath skirting the premises
and curving across a paddock to arrive on
Holly Lane.

Turn right, noticing the entrance to
Gorse Hill Nature Reserve. The walk later
crosses sections of the reserve, but if you
have time, it's worth exploring the visitor
centre and Cabin Wood (limited opening).
The reserve has developed an impressive
diversity of habitat in its 35 hectares,
including native woodland, wetland,
ponds, a hay meadow and an orchard.
Follow Holly Lane past a row of cottages
and, at the end of the road, keep straight
ahead past the iron gate, another entrance
to the nature reserve. Bear left along a

Narrow Lane Farm

◄ Gorse Hill Nature Reserve

0   1km

Clieves Hills Farm

Booth's Farm

Gorse Hill Nature Reserve

Devil's Wall

Gaw Hill

To Burscough

Clieves Hills Lane

Fir Tree Lane

Booth's Lane

The Hollies

Holly Lane

Clieves Hills

Small Lane

Ormskirk

A59

To Formby

To Maghull

lovely public footpath, enclosed by hedges and shaded by trees. Red campion, forget-me-nots and bluebells fill the verges in season. At a T-junction, turn right onto a track around the wood and emerge from the trees to cross a ditch. Cross over the next field and you come to Booth's Lane.

Turn right for 200m, then left on a footpath opposite Owls Barn. Traverse the field and turn left to follow the next road, Fir Tree Lane, for 400m. At the junction with Small Lane, turn right along a track amidst arable land. At the far end, pass a house and turn right onto a road, climbing this to the top of the hill. A couple of seats offer a panoramic view across the coastal plain as far as Liverpool, Cheshire, North Wales and even the Lake District on a clear day. If you are so inclined, you can even look out for Blackpool Tower! Curve round to the end

of Clieves Hills Lane and at the T-junction turn left. Follow the lane to the next crossroads. Keep straight ahead here, but only for a few metres, before going to the right into the driveway of Clieves Hill farmhouse. The path weaves past an unusual brick towered house and continues across fields to join a road on the apex of a bend.

Keep straight ahead here for 200m, then turn right onto a track. Wiggle past a couple of ponds and gently ascend the slope of Gaw Hill. Go through a gate to the nature reserve on the left and rise to the top of the hill, capped by an open meadow. Look out for a gap to the left and find a path rising between hawthorn trees. It follows the boundary of the reservoir compound until it meets the access track. Follow this back to the start at Christ Church.

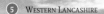

Freshfield Dunes

Distance 8km **Time** 3 hours
Terrain level paths together with sections
across sand dunes and along the beach
Map OS Explorer 285 **Access** frequent
trains from Liverpool and Southport
serve Freshfield Station

The Sefton Coast has been created by wind
and tide moulding a vast system of sand
dunes, anchored by marram grass and
blanketed with pinewoods. Uncommon
species like the Natterjack toad call this
home, along with a variety of butterflies
and a colony of red squirrels. Apart from
the sand dunes, also known as the Formby
Hills, the landscape is almost completely
flat as the West Lancashire plain stretches
to meet the Irish Sea. This walk is entirely
within the county of Merseyside on the
narrow coastal strip which reaches north
to Southport. The circuit is level, reaching
the dizzying height of 15m above sea level,
but it's full of interest and diversity.

From Freshfield Station, go north along
Montague Road for the Fisherman's Path,
alongside the station car park and parallel
to the railway. Where the road ends keep
straight ahead on the track, skirting silver
birch woodland, emblazoned with
patches of bright yellow broom in season.
Around 1km from the start, turn left over
the railway on a level crossing and follow
the driveway through the golf course,
known as the Fisherman's Path. Pass
through a gate to enter Ainsdale Dunes
National Nature Reserve.

Keep straight ahead here, staying on
the Fisherman's Path, now marked by red-
topped posts as it travels into a vast sand
dune system colonised by mature pine
and silver birch trees. The main path
peters out in a clearing at the foot of the
open dunes. Carry straight on ahead,
crossing the dunes on a sandy path,
before coming to the vast level expanse
of the beach. Even at sea level, the views

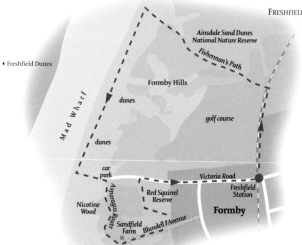

◀ Freshfield Dunes

Ainsdale Sand Dunes
National Nature Reserve

Fisherman's Path

Formby Hills

dunes

Mad Wharf

dunes

golf course

car
park

Victoria Road

Freshfield
Station

Asparagus Route

Red Squirrel
Reserve

Nicotine
Wood

Sandfield
Farm

Blundell Avenue

Formby

stretch out to North Wales and along the Lancashire coast.

Turn left and follow the foreshore for about 2km. It is a safe and clear route close to the dunes and refuge can be sought here easily but be aware of the high tidal range and exercise due caution away from the edge. Continue until you reach the tall marker post for Victoria Road. Turn left here and follow the broad sandy path into the car park. (To shorten the walk just walk along the access road and head for the station.)

At the far side of the car park, next to an information panel, find the waymarked Asparagus Trail. This is so called because the crop was grown as a speciality by local farms, benefiting from the sandy well-drained soil. The path weaves between the dunes and fields, passing through Nicotine Wood. Stay on the main route, indicated by markers and later passing the former asparagus fields.

At a T-junction, turn left and walk along the tarmac drive, passing the National Trust countryside depot. Soon after a slight rise, watch out for a marker post directing the Asparagus Trail left into the woods. The path now meanders through long-established sand dunes, dominated by mature pine trees. A short distance further on, where the track turns left, keep straight ahead through a gate into a picnic area. On the far side continue over the bank to reach the main access drive. Turn right to follow this back to the exit of the National Trust site. Just before the exit barrier, there is a short circular walk on the right, touring the red squirrel reserve. Then it's a straightforward walk along Victoria Road back to Freshfield Station.

Index